Your Digital Fortress: A Comprehensive Guide to Cybersecurity for Home Users

Table Of Contents

Introduction

When we think of cybersecurity and cybercrimes, we often associate those words with the business world. Still, in an era where our homes are more connected than ever, the need for a robust defense against digital threats has never been more critical. "Digital Fortress: A Comprehensive Guide to Cybersecurity for Home Users" is a beacon of knowledge designed to empower you, the homeowner, with the tools and understanding to safeguard your digital domain.

As we navigate the vast and complex landscape of the digital frontier, our homes have become the battleground for a new kind of warfare – one waged by invisible foes in the realms of cyberspace. Cybersecurity is no longer the sole concern of governments and corporations; it is a personal imperative for everyone who relies on the Internet for communication, work, education, and entertainment.

This book is your comprehensive guide through the intricacies of securing your home network against the ever-evolving threats lurking in the digital shadows. As you read this guide, you'll encounter instances of repetition of key concepts; rest assured, concepts repeated more than once herein are essential. This guide is not a comprehensive "How-To" book; it is meant to provide information on the cybersecurity landscape and reveal best practices. Some of the concepts herein are what I would consider "extra mile" practices meant to provide an indepth understanding of the best cybersecurity practices. While no system is 100% secure, as even government organizations get infiltrated, my goal is to equip the average home user with the knowledge needed to help mitigate any potential digital intrusion. From understanding the lay of the land to building formidable defenses, each chapter is a stepping stone toward creating a relatively impenetrable fortress around your digital life.

Let's dig in.

Chapter 1: The Digital Frontier - Understanding the Cybersecurity Landscape

Cybersecurity has become more critical than ever in the ever-expanding digital landscape, where our lives intertwine with technology. This chapter is a foundational exploration into cybersecurity, providing average home users with the essential knowledge needed to navigate and secure their digital presence. From the evolving threat landscape to the fundamental principles of cybersecurity, this chapter aims to empower readers with a comprehensive understanding of the challenges and strategies at play in digital security.

1.1 The Evolution of the Cybersecurity Landscape

The digital frontier has witnessed a rapid evolution from the early days of personal computing to our interconnected world. As our reliance on digital technologies has grown, so has the sophistication of cyber threats. Understanding the historical context of cybersecurity is crucial for appreciating the current challenges and anticipating future developments.

In the nascent stages of the internet, cybersecurity primarily focused on protecting individual computers from viruses and malware. As connectivity increased, so did the scale and complexity of cyber threats. Social media, cloud computing, and the Internet of Things (IoT) introduced new dimensions to cybersecurity, expanding the potential attack surface.

1.2 The Pervasiveness of Cyber Threats

Cyber threats have evolved from simple viruses to complex and targeted attacks that compromise personal information, financial assets, and national security. Average home users are not exempt from these threats, as cybercriminals often target individuals for various reasons, including identity theft, financial gain, or unauthorized access to sensitive data.

- Malware: Malicious software, or malware, remains a pervasive threat; this includes viruses, ransomware, and spyware designed to infiltrate and compromise systems.
- Phishing: Phishing attacks involve deceptive tactics to trick individuals into revealing sensitive information, often through fake websites or emails that appear legitimate.
- Identity Theft: Cybercriminals may steal personal information to impersonate individuals, leading to potential financial loss and reputational damage.
- Data Breaches: Large-scale data breaches compromise the security of personal and financial information, affecting millions of individuals.
- Understanding the variety and motivations behind cyber threats is the first step toward building a proactive cybersecurity mindset.

1.3 The Human Element: A Key Factor in Cybersecurity

While technological advancements are crucial in cybersecurity, the human element remains significant. Average home users are often the targets of social engineering tactics, where cybercriminals exploit human behavior to gain access to sensitive information.

- Social Engineering: Techniques such as pretexting, baiting, and quid pro quo rely on manipulating individuals through psychological manipulation rather than exploiting technical vulnerabilities.
- User Awareness: Educating users about common social engineering tactics empowers them to recognize and resist manipulation attempts, contributing to a more resilient cybersecurity posture.

1.4 Cybersecurity as a Shared Responsibility

In the digital age, cybersecurity is a shared responsibility beyond individual users. Governments, businesses, and technology providers are crucial in creating a secure online environment. Understanding the collaborative nature of cybersecurity helps users recognize the support systems in place and navigate the complex network of stakeholders.

- Government Regulations: Governments enact cybersecurity regulations and standards to protect citizens and ensure the secure operation of critical infrastructure.
- Corporate Security Measures: Businesses implement cybersecurity measures to safeguard customer data, financial assets, and proprietary information; this includes encryption, access controls, and regular security audits.
- Technology Provider Safeguards: Technology companies continuously develop security features and updates to protect users from emerging threats. Keeping software and devices up to date is fundamental to user-side cybersecurity.

1.5 Key Principles of Cybersecurity for Home Users

Empowering average home users in cybersecurity involves distilling complex concepts into actionable principles. The following fundamental principles serve as a foundation for a secure digital experience:

Principle 1: Awareness and Education: Stay informed about current cyber threats and educate yourself on best practices for digital safety. Knowledge is a powerful tool in the fight against cybercrime.

Principle 2: Strong and Unique Passwords: Create strong, unique passwords for each online account. Utilize a combination of letters, numbers, and special characters, and avoid using easily guessable information.

Principle 3: Multi-Factor Authentication (MFA): Enable MFA whenever possible to add an extra layer of security beyond passwords. MFA requires multiple forms of verification, enhancing the overall security of your accounts.

Principle 4: Regular Software Updates: Keep your operating system, applications, and antivirus programs current. Software updates often include security patches that address vulnerabilities.

Principle 5: Vigilance Against Phishing: Be cautious of unsolicited emails, messages, or links. Verify the legitimacy of communications before clicking on links or providing sensitive information.

Principle 6: Secure Wi-Fi Practices: Secure your home Wi-Fi network with a strong password, and regularly update the router firmware. Avoid public Wi-Fi for sensitive transactions.

Principle 7: Backup Your Data: Regularly backup essential data to an external drive or a secure cloud service. In the event of a ransomware attack or hardware failure, backups ensure data recovery.

1.6 Cybersecurity Tools for Home Users

Arming oneself with the right cybersecurity tools is integral to building a robust defense against online threats. While the market offers many options, understanding the essential tools tailored for average home users is critical.

- Antivirus Software: A reliable program that protects against malware, viruses, and other malicious software. Choose reputable software with real-time scanning capabilities.
- Password Managers: Password managers simplify the management of complex and unique passwords. They securely store passwords, generate strong ones, and streamline the login process.
- Virtual Private Network (VPN): A VPN encrypts internet traffic, enhancing online privacy and security. It is precious when using public Wi-Fi networks.
- Firewalls: act as barriers between your device and the internet, monitoring and controlling incoming and outgoing network traffic. Most operating systems have built-in firewalls that can be enabled for added security.

1.7 Emerging Trends in Cybersecurity

As technology continues to advance, so do the strategies and tactics employed by cybercriminals. Staying abreast of emerging trends is crucial for adapting cybersecurity measures accordingly.

- Artificial Intelligence (AI) in Cybersecurity: Defenders and attackers increasingly leverage AI. AI-powered cybersecurity tools can analyze vast datasets to identify and respond to threats in real-time.
- Ransomware-as-a-Service (RaaS): Ransomware attacks have become more sophisticated, with some attackers offering RaaS, enabling even those with minimal technical skills to launch ransomware campaigns.
- Internet of Things (IoT) Security: The proliferation of IoT devices introduces new security challenges. Securing smart home devices and understanding their potential vulnerabilities is crucial.

1.8 The Intersection of Privacy and Cybersecurity

Privacy and cybersecurity are intertwined, with each influencing the other. As users strive to protect their digital assets, they must also be mindful of preserving their privacy rights.

- Data Protection Regulations: Privacy laws and regulations, such as the General Data Protection Regulation (GDPR), aim to protect individuals' data and privacy rights. Understanding these regulations is vital for users and businesses alike.
- User Privacy Settings: Adjust privacy settings on online platforms and devices to control the amount of personal information shared. Regularly review and update these settings to align with evolving preferences.

1.9 The Role of Cyber Hygiene in Digital Wellness

Cyber hygiene encompasses the practices and habits contributing to a healthy and secure digital lifestyle. Like personal hygiene, maintaining cyber hygiene is essential for preventing digital infections.

- Device Clean-Up: Regularly declutter devices by removing unused apps and files; this improves device performance and reduces the attack surface for potential threats.
- Email Management: Keep email inboxes organized and regularly review and delete unnecessary emails. Be cautious of email attachments and links, especially from unknown or suspicious sources.
- Social Media Clean-Up: Review and adjust privacy settings on social media platforms. Consider limiting the personal information shared publicly and regularly auditing friend lists.

1.10 Conclusion: Navigating the Cybersecurity Frontier

As we conclude this introductory journey into the digital frontier of cybersecurity, it's clear that the landscape is vast, dynamic, and requires constant vigilance. The principles, tools, and trends explored here serve as a foundation for the chapters to come, where we will delve deeper into specific aspects of cybersecurity tailored for average home users.

In the forthcoming chapters, we will explore securing personal devices, protecting online identities, and cultivating a resilient cybersecurity mindset. Every fragment of knowledge gained is a step toward a safer and more confident digital existence. Embrace the evolving nature of the digital frontier, and let the insights shared here be your guiding compass in cybersecurity's vast and ever-changing realm.

Chapter 2: Building Fortifications - Securing Your Home Network

In the digital age, your home network is the bedrock of your online presence, connecting devices and facilitating the flow of information. This chapter is dedicated to unraveling the intricacies of home network security, providing average home users with the knowledge and tools needed to fortify their digital domains. From understanding the components of a home network to implementing robust security measures, this exploration aims to empower readers to create a resilient defense against cyber threats.

2.1 The Home Network Ecosystem
Your home network is a dynamic ecosystem comprising various devices with unique roles and vulnerabilities. From smartphones and laptops to smart TVs and IoT devices, the interconnectedness of these devices necessitates a holistic approach to security.
Components of a Home Network:

- Router: The central hub that connects devices to the internet and facilitates communication.
- Modem: Bridges the gap between your home network and the internet service provider (ISP).
- Devices: Including computers, smartphones, tablets, smart home devices, and more.

Understanding the roles of these components is fundamental to implementing effective security measures.

2.2 The Role of the Router in Home Network Security
The router stands as the guardian at the gateway of your home network, making it a primary focus for fortification. A secure router is crucial for preventing unauthorized access and protecting sensitive data.

- Default Credentials: Change the default username and password for your router. Default credentials are well-known to attackers, making them easily exploitable.

- Encryption Protocols: Enable WPA3 encryption for Wi-Fi networks; this ensures that the data transmitted between devices and the router is secure and resistant to eavesdropping.
- Firmware Updates: Regularly update the router firmware to patch vulnerabilities. Check for updates on the router manufacturer's website or use the router's admin interface.

2.3 Strengthening Wi-Fi Security

Wi-Fi is the lifeblood of home connectivity, but its signals can extend beyond the walls of your home, presenting opportunities for unauthorized access. Strengthening Wi-Fi security is essential for maintaining the integrity of your home network.

- Unique SSID and Password: Change the default Service Set Identifier (SSID) to a unique name and use a strong, unique Wi-Fi password. Avoid using easily guessable information.
- Guest Network: If your router supports it, set up a guest network for visitors; this separates guest devices from your primary network, adding an extra layer of security.
- Wi-Fi Protected Access (WPA) Settings: Use the latest WPA protocol supported by your devices. WPA3 is the most secure option, but WPA2 remains a strong choice if WPA3 is unavailable.

2.4 Device Security on the Home Network

Every device connected to your home network is a potential entry point for cyber threats. Security measures at the device level are crucial for a comprehensive defense strategy.

- Device Updates: Regularly update the operating systems and software on all connected devices. Updates often include security patches that address known vulnerabilities.
- Antivirus and Anti-malware Software: Install reputable antivirus and anti-malware software on computers and other devices. Keep these programs updated to defend against the latest threats.
- Firewall Protection: Enable firewalls on individual devices, if available. Firewalls monitor and control incoming and outgoing network traffic, adding an extra layer of defense.

2.5 IoT Devices: Balancing Convenience and Security

The proliferation of IoT devices, from smart thermostats to connected cameras, brings unparalleled convenience and introduces security challenges. Securing IoT devices is critical to prevent them from becoming entry points for cyber attackers.

- Change Default Credentials: Many IoT devices come with default usernames and passwords. Change these credentials to unique and strong ones to prevent unauthorized access.
- Isolate IoT Devices: Segregate IoT devices on a separate network; this limits their ability to communicate directly with more sensitive devices on the leading network.

- Regular Updates: Ensure that IoT devices receive firmware and software updates promptly. Manufacturers often release patches to address security vulnerabilities.

2.6 Network Monitoring and Intrusion Detection

Vigilant monitoring of your home network is a proactive approach to identifying and mitigating potential security threats. Implementing intrusion detection measures enhances your ability to respond to suspicious activities.

- Network Monitoring Tools: Utilize network monitoring tools to keep track of the devices connected to your network, monitor data traffic, and identify anomalies.
- Intrusion Detection Systems (IDS): IDS can alert you to potential security incidents by analyzing network traffic for signs of malicious activity. Some modern routers come with built-in IDS features.
- Regular Audits: Conduct periodic audits of connected devices and their security settings. Remove any unknown or unauthorized devices from the network.

2.7 Virtual Private Network (VPN) for Enhanced Privacy

A Virtual Private Network (VPN) is a powerful tool for enhancing the privacy and security of your internet connection. It encrypts your internet traffic, making monitoring your online activities more challenging for third parties.

- VPN Setup: Choose a reputable VPN service and follow their setup instructions. Many VPNs offer user-friendly apps for various devices.
- Use on Public Networks: When connecting to public Wi-Fi networks, use a VPN to secure your internet connection and protect your data from potential eavesdropping.
- Device Compatibility: Ensure that the VPN service is compatible with all the devices you use on your home network, including computers, smartphones, and smart TVs.

2.8 Parental Controls: Safeguarding Family Internet Use

For households with children, implementing parental controls is crucial for managing and monitoring online activities. Parental control features are often built into routers or configured through third-party software.

- Content Filtering: Enable content filtering to block access to inappropriate websites or content based on predefined categories.
- Time Limits: Set time limits for internet usage, helping to balance online and offline activities and promote a healthy digital lifestyle.

- Device-Specific Controls: Some routers allow you to apply controls per device, providing granular control over each user's internet access.

2.9 Secure Remote Access: Balancing Convenience and Security

As remote work and digital collaboration become more prevalent, ensuring secure remote access to your home network is vital. Implementing certain practices prevents unauthorized access and protects sensitive information.

- Virtual Private Network (VPN): When accessing your home network remotely, use a VPN to establish a secure and encrypted connection.
- Two-Factor Authentication (2FA): Enable 2FA for remote access if your router supports it; this adds a layer of verification beyond the standard username and password.
- Strong Remote Passwords: Use a robust and unique password if your router allows remote access. Avoid default credentials, and consider changing the remote access port for added security.

2.10 Regular Security Audits: A Habit of Vigilance

Fortifying your home network is an ongoing process that requires regular evaluation and adjustment. Implementing routine security audits ensures that your defenses remain robust and adaptive to emerging threats.

- Scheduled Audits: Establish a schedule for network security audits, during which you review router settings, check for firmware updates, and assess the security configurations of connected devices.
- Check for Rogue Devices: Periodically scan for rogue devices on your network that may have gained unauthorized access. Remove any unfamiliar or suspicious devices promptly.
- Password Changes: Change your router password and Wi-Fi password periodically. This practice reduces the risk of unauthorized access and enhances overall network security.

2.11 Conclusion: Fortifying Your Digital Stronghold

As we conclude this exploration into securing your home network, envision your digital domain as a stronghold that stands resilient against the ever-evolving landscape of cyber threats. By implementing the strategies outlined in this chapter, you fortify the walls of your home network, creating a secure environment for your digital activities.

In the upcoming chapters, we will continue to build upon this foundation, exploring additional dimensions of cybersecurity tailored for average home users. Each measure adopted, each fortification reinforced, contributes to a safer and more confident digital existence. Let the knowledge gained here be the shield that guards your digital stronghold in the vast and interconnected world of the internet.

Chapter 3: Guardians at the Gate - Passwords and Authentication

In the digital realm, passwords serve as the frontline guardians, standing at the gate of our online lives. This chapter delves deep into passwords and authentication, unraveling the intricacies of securing your digital presence. For average home users, understanding the importance of strong passwords, exploring multi-factor authentication, and navigating the landscape of secure access are essential steps toward fortifying the gateway to their digital world.

3.1 The Password Paradox: Balancing Security and Convenience

Passwords are the keys that unlock the digital doors that guard access to personal emails, social media accounts, and online banking. Striking a balance between security and convenience is the first challenge in the password paradox.

- Password Complexity: Craft passwords that are complex and resistant to brute force attacks. A mix of uppercase and lowercase letters, numbers, and special characters enhances security.
- Memorability: Despite the complexity, passwords should be memorable. Avoid using easily guessable information, such as birthdays or common words, while ensuring you can easily recall them.
- Unique for Each Account: The cardinal rule of password management is to use unique passwords for each account; this prevents a security breach on one platform from compromising others.

3.2 The Anatomy of a Strong Password

Creating a solid password involves more than just choosing random characters. Understanding the elements contributing to password strength is pivotal for crafting robust and resilient access credentials.

- Passphrases: Consider using a passphrase—sequences of words or sentences such as "Bird_Dog_Cloud_Bike" or "I_Love_Chocolate_Sundays." These are easier to remember and can be as secure as traditional passwords when well-constructed.
- Avoiding Predictable Patterns: Steer clear of using easily guessable patterns or information, such as sequential numbers, common phrases, or keyboard patterns. Predictability is the enemy of security.

- Length Matters: Longer passwords are generally more secure. Aim for a minimum length of 12 characters; the longer, the better. Longer passwords increase the complexity and time required for brute-force attacks.

3.3 Password Hygiene: Nurturing Good Practices

Maintaining good password hygiene involves adopting practices that contribute to the overall security of your digital accounts. From regular updates to avoiding common pitfalls, cultivating these habits is essential.

- Regular Updates: Set a schedule for password updates. This practice reduces the risk of unauthorized access and ensures that your passwords remain resilient against evolving cyber threats.
- Avoiding Personal Information: Refrain from using easily obtainable personal information, such as your name, birth date, or address. This information is often the first target for attackers attempting to guess passwords.
- Beware of Phishing: Be vigilant against phishing attempts. Avoid clicking on links in suspicious emails, and always verify the authenticity of websites before entering your password.

3.4 Multi-Factor Authentication (MFA): Enhancing Security Layers

Recognizing the limitations of passwords alone, multi-factor authentication (MFA) is a powerful ally. MFA adds an extra layer of protection beyond the traditional username and password, significantly enhancing security.

- Something You Know: The traditional password falls into this category.
- Something You Have: This could be a security token, a smart card, a USB drive, or a verification code sent to your mobile device.
- Something You Are: Biometric data, such as fingerprints or facial recognition, is increasingly used for authentication.

3.5 Navigating the Landscape of Biometric Authentication

Biometric authentication represents a leap forward in user-friendly and secure access. As the technology becomes more prevalent, understanding its nuances and considerations is crucial for average home users.

- Fingerprint Recognition: Many modern smartphones and laptops come equipped with fingerprint scanners. Enabling this feature provides a convenient and secure method of unlocking devices.

- Facial Recognition: Facial recognition technology, while convenient, requires robust security measures. Ensure that the facial recognition system resists spoofing attempts using photos or videos.
- Retina Scans and Voice Recognition: High-security environments may employ retina scans or voice recognition for authentication. These methods are more sophisticated and less common for average home users.

3.6 Choosing and Using a Password Manager

Managing a multitude of complex and unique passwords can be overwhelming. Enter password managers—a beacon of convenience and security for the average home user.

- Secure Storage: Password managers securely store your login credentials in an encrypted vault; this protects your passwords from unauthorized access.
- Password Generator: Most password managers include a password generator that creates strong, random passwords for your accounts; this eliminates the need to devise and remember complex passwords manually.
- Synchronization Across Devices: Password managers often sync across various devices, ensuring your passwords are accessible and updated on all your devices.

3.7 Mastering Password Recovery Without Compromising Security

Password recovery mechanisms are essential for regaining access to accounts in case of forgotten passwords. However, striking the right balance between accessibility and security is crucial.

- Alternative Email or Phone: Many platforms offer password recovery through secondary email addresses or phone numbers. Ensure that these recovery options are secure and regularly updated.
- Security Questions: Be cautious with security questions, as the answers may be accessible or guessable. Opt for questions with answers that are not publicly available or use customized questions.
- Two-Factor Authentication for Recovery: Some platforms allow you to use two-factor authentication for password recovery; this adds an extra layer of security to the recovery process.

3.8 Educating Family Members on Password Practices

In a household, the strength of cybersecurity is only as robust as its weakest link. Educating family members on password practices ensures a unified and secure digital environment.

- Family Password Policies: Establish family password policies that emphasize unique passwords for each member, regular updates, and the use of password managers.
- Password Manager Training: Familiarize family members with password managers, guiding them on how to use these tools effectively for secure password management.
- Educate about MFA: Share the importance of Multi-Factor Authentication with family members and assist them in enabling MFA for their accounts.

3.9 Password Security on Mobile Devices
Mobile devices play a central role in our digital lives; securing passwords on these devices is paramount. Implementing password security measures on mobile devices contributes to a comprehensive cybersecurity strategy.

- Biometric Authentication: Leverage biometric authentication features, such as fingerprint scanning or facial recognition, on your mobile device for secure and convenient access.
- Secure Password Managers on Mobile: Use reputable password manager apps on your mobile device. Ensure that these apps support encryption and have a fast login process.
- App Permissions: Review and manage app permissions on your mobile device, especially those related to password managers. Grant only the necessary permissions to enhance security.

3.10 Password Security for Children: Instilling Good Habits
In a digital age where children are active users of online platforms, instilling good password habits early on is crucial for their digital safety.

- Educational Games: Introduce educational games that teach children the importance of strong and unique passwords. Make learning about cybersecurity engaging and age-appropriate.
- Parental Controls: Implement parental controls on devices used by children; this includes setting up secure passwords for parental control settings and educating children about responsible online behavior.
- Supervised Password Creation: Supervise and assist children in creating their passwords for accounts related to educational platforms or games. Use this opportunity to educate them about password security.

3.11 Periodic Password Audits: Maintaining Vigilance
The digital landscape is dynamic, and periodic password audits are essential for maintaining the security of your accounts. Regularly reviewing and updating passwords contributes to an adaptive and resilient cybersecurity strategy.

- Scheduled Audits: Establish a schedule for password audits, during which you review and update passwords for your accounts; this ensures that your digital defenses remain robust.
- Check for Breaches: Use online tools to check whether your email addresses or passwords are compromised in data breaches. If compromised, take immediate action to update passwords.
- Password Expiration Policies: Some password managers offer features that remind users to update their passwords regularly. Consider enabling this feature for added security.

3.12 Secure Handling of Password Resets: Mitigating Risks

Password resets are a common practice for regaining access to accounts but pose security risks. Mitigating these risks involves adopting secure practices when initiating or responding to password reset requests.

- Verify Email Communications: Verify the sender's legitimacy when receiving an email about a password reset. Avoid clicking on email links and visit the platform's official website to initiate the reset.
- Use Secure Channels: Use secure channels such as official websites or mobile apps when initiating a password reset. Avoid using links in emails, as they may lead to phishing sites.
- Monitor Account Activity: After a password reset, monitor your account activity for suspicious behavior. Some platforms provide notifications for account access or changes, which can alert you to potential threats.

3.13 Password Security and the Internet of Things (IoT)

Securing passwords becomes imperative as our homes become more interconnected through IoT devices. The following considerations apply to password security in the IoT era:

- Change Default Passwords: Many IoT devices come with default passwords. Change these passwords immediately to prevent unauthorized access, as default passwords are often well-known.
- Use Strong Passwords for IoT Apps: If your IoT devices connect to mobile apps, ensure that the passwords for these apps are solid and unique. Consider using a password manager for added security.
- Regularly Update Device Firmware: Keep your IoT devices up to date by installing firmware updates. These updates often include security patches that address vulnerabilities.

3.14 Conclusion: Crafting a Robust Password Strategy

As we conclude this exploration into password management, envision your passwords as strings of characters and guardians of your digital realm. By adopting strong and unique passwords, leveraging password managers, and embracing multi-factor authentication, you fortify the gateway to your digital world.

In the forthcoming chapters, we will continue to build upon this foundation, exploring additional dimensions of cybersecurity for home users. Each secure password and vigilant update contributes to the resilience of your digital defenses. This shield stands firm in the face of evolving cyber threats. Let the knowledge gained here be the key that unlocks a secure and confident journey through the vast landscapes of the digital realm.

Chapter 4: Sentinels in the Shadows - Antivirus and Anti-malware Strategies

In the ever-expanding digital landscape, where every click and download carries potential risks, having vigilant sentinels in the form of antivirus and anti-malware tools is paramount. This chapter delves into digital guardianship, exploring the strategies and best practices for selecting, deploying, and maintaining effective antivirus and anti-malware defenses. For average home users, understanding the nuances of these cybersecurity tools is crucial in fortifying their digital strongholds against the unseen threats lurking in the shadows.

4.1 The Imperative of Antivirus and Anti-malware Defense

As technology advances, so do the threats that seek to exploit vulnerabilities in our digital ecosystems. Antivirus and anti-malware tools are the first line of defense against a myriad of malicious software designed to infiltrate, compromise, and exploit our devices and data.

- Defining Malicious Software: Malicious software, or malware, is a broad term encompassing various harmful programs, including viruses, worms, trojans, ransomware, spyware, and adware. Each poses unique risks and challenges, necessitating a multi-faceted defense strategy.
- Antivirus vs. Anti-malware: While the terms are often used interchangeably, there are distinctions between antivirus and anti-malware tools. Antivirus traditionally focuses on preventing, detecting, and removing viruses, whereas anti-malware encompasses a broader range of malicious software.

4.2 Understanding the Threat Landscape

Before delving into the selection and deployment of antivirus and anti-malware tools, it's crucial to comprehend the diverse landscape of cyber threats. Each type of malware operates with distinct objectives and methods, making a nuanced understanding essential for effective defense.

- Viruses: Self-replicating programs that attach to clean files, spreading from one host to another.

- Worms: Independent programs that replicate and spread across networks, often exploiting vulnerabilities to propagate.
- Trojans: trojans deceive users into unwittingly installing malicious programs by disguising them as legitimate software,
- Ransomware: Encrypts files or systems, demanding payment for their release.
- Spyware: Secretly monitors user activities, collecting sensitive information without consent.
- Adware: Displays unwanted advertisements, often bundled with free software.

Understanding the characteristics and behaviors of these threats informs the selection of security tools tailored to combat them effectively.

4.3 Choosing an Antivirus or Anti-malware Solution

Selecting the proper antivirus or anti-malware solution is a critical decision requiring consideration of various factors. With many options available, average home users must navigate the landscape to find a solution that aligns with their needs and provides robust protection.

- Reputation and Reviews: Research the reputation and reviews of antivirus and anti-malware products. Look for independent assessments and user feedback to gauge effectiveness and user-friendliness.
- Features and Capabilities: Assess the features and capabilities of each solution. Consider real-time scanning, heuristic analysis, behavior monitoring, and additional security layers.
- Resource Utilization: Evaluate the impact of the antivirus or anti-malware software on system resources. Balancing adequate protection with minimal performance impact is crucial for a positive user experience.
- Compatibility: Ensure the chosen solution is compatible with your operating system and other software. Some antivirus programs may have compatibility issues with specific applications or versions.

4.4 Real-time Scanning and Heuristic Analysis

Two key features distinguish effective antivirus and anti-malware tools: real-time scanning and heuristic analysis. These components work in tandem to identify and neutralize threats as they emerge.

- Real-time Scanning: This feature monitors files and processes in real-time, immediately flagging or blocking any suspicious activity. It provides instantaneous protection against known threats.

- Heuristic Analysis: Heuristic analysis involves identifying potentially malicious behavior based on patterns and characteristics rather than relying solely on known signatures. This proactive approach enhances the ability to detect new and evolving threats.

4.5 Behavioral Monitoring and Zero-Day Threats

The landscape of cyber threats is dynamic, with new threats emerging regularly. Behavioral monitoring and the ability to combat zero-day threats are integral components of a robust antivirus and anti-malware defense strategy.

- Behavioral Monitoring: This feature observes the behavior of programs and processes on a system, identifying anomalous or malicious activities. It is particularly effective against threats with polymorphic or changing characteristics.
- Zero-Day Threats: Zero-day threats exploit vulnerabilities without a patch or defense mechanism. Antivirus solutions with proactive heuristic analysis and behavioral monitoring are crucial for identifying and mitigating these threats.

4.6 Automatic Updates and Threat Intelligence

Staying ahead of the ever-evolving threat landscape requires continuous updates and access to threat intelligence. Antivirus and anti-malware solutions offering automatic updates and leveraging threat intelligence databases provide a dynamic defense against emerging threats.

- Automatic Updates: Regular updates ensure the antivirus software has the latest threat signatures and security patches. Automatic updates reduce the risk of vulnerabilities and enhance the solution's overall effectiveness.
- Threat Intelligence: Antivirus solutions that leverage threat intelligence databases benefit from a collective knowledge base. These databases compile information about new threats, attack vectors, and vulnerabilities, contributing to a more informed and adaptive defense.

4.7 Adapting to Evolving Threats: Machine Learning and AI

As cyber threats become more sophisticated, antivirus and anti-malware tools increasingly incorporate machine learning and artificial intelligence (AI) to enhance their capabilities.

- Machine Learning: Machine learning algorithms analyze patterns and data to improve threat detection accuracy. This adaptive approach allows antivirus tools to recognize and respond to new threats based on learned behavior.
- Artificial Intelligence: AI algorithms can analyze large datasets rapidly, identifying trends and anomalies. In antivirus software, AI contributes to faster and more efficient threat detection.

4.8 Supplementary Security Measures

While antivirus and anti-malware tools play a central role in defense, adopting supplementary security measures enhances overall protection. Average home users should consider incorporating the following practices into their cybersecurity strategy:

- Firewalls: Activate firewalls on your devices and network to monitor and control incoming and outgoing traffic. Firewalls add a layer of defense, complementing the role of antivirus software.
- Regular Backups: Create regular backups of essential data. In the event of a malware attack, having a recent backup ensures that you can restore your files without paying a ransom.
- Security Awareness Training: Stay informed about cybersecurity threats and best practices. Security awareness training empowers users to recognize and avoid potential risks, reducing the likelihood of falling victim to phishing or other social engineering attacks.

4.9 Best Practices for Antivirus and Anti-malware Hygiene

Effectiveness in combating cyber threats relies on the choice of antivirus tools and implementing good hygiene practices. These best practices contribute to a holistic approach to digital security:

- Regular Scans: Conduct regular full-system scans in addition to real-time scanning. Full-system scans are more thorough and can identify deeply embedded or dormant threats.
- Prompt Action on Threat Alerts: Take immediate action in response to alerts from your antivirus software. Quarantine or remove detected threats promptly to prevent further damage.
- Scheduled Scans: Set up scheduled scans during periods of lower device usage, ensuring that antivirus scans do not interfere with everyday activities.

4.10 Antivirus and Anti-malware on Multiple Devices

In a connected world, where individuals use multiple devices for work, leisure, and communication, extending antivirus and anti-malware protection to all devices is essential.

- Cross-Platform Compatibility: Choose antivirus solutions that offer cross-platform compatibility, ensuring protection across various operating systems, including Windows, macOS, Android, and iOS.
- Unified Management: Some antivirus solutions provide centralized management interfaces, allowing users to monitor and control the security of multiple devices from a single dashboard.

4.11 Evaluating Free vs. Paid Antivirus Solutions

Choosing between free and paid antivirus solutions is a common dilemma for users. While free options provide baseline protection, paid solutions often offer additional features and enhanced security.

- Free Antivirus Solutions: Suitable for essential protection, free antivirus solutions can be effective for average home users with standard usage patterns. However, they may need more advanced features present in paid alternatives.
- Paid Antivirus Solutions: Paid options often include additional layers of protection, advanced threat detection mechanisms, and priority customer support. Consider the specific needs of your digital activities when evaluating paid solutions.

4.12 Troubleshooting and Support

Even with robust antivirus and anti-malware defenses, occasional issues may arise. Understanding troubleshooting steps and accessing reliable support channels is essential for resolving problems promptly.

- Online Knowledge Base: Antivirus providers often maintain online knowledge bases with articles and guides to help users troubleshoot common issues independently.
- Customer Support: Evaluate the customer support options provided by antivirus vendors. Some offer email support, live chat, or phone support to assist users with more complex issues.

4.13 Antivirus and Anti-malware for Email Security

Email remains a primary vector for malware distribution, making email security a critical component of overall antivirus and anti-malware defenses.

- Email Scanning: Ensure that your antivirus solution includes email scanning capabilities. This feature examines attachments and links in incoming and outgoing emails for potential threats.
- Phishing Protection: Some antivirus tools incorporate phishing protection features to identify and block email phishing attempts; this helps users avoid falling victim to deceptive schemes.

4.14 Mobile Security and Antivirus Apps

As mobile devices become integral to our daily lives, extending antivirus protection to smartphones and tablets is imperative.

- Mobile Antivirus Apps: Choose reputable antivirus apps designed for mobile devices. These apps provide real-time scanning, threat detection, and additional security features tailored for mobile platforms.
- App Permissions: Review and manage app permissions on your mobile device, especially those related to antivirus apps. Grant only the necessary permissions to enhance security.

4.15 Conclusion: Fortifying the Digital Perimeter

In cybersecurity, where threats continuously evolve, antivirus and anti-malware tools serve as the vigilant sentinels protecting the digital perimeter of our lives. By understanding the threat landscape, selecting effective solutions, and incorporating best practices, average home users can fortify their digital strongholds against the unseen adversaries that lurk in the shadows.

In the upcoming chapters, we will explore nuanced aspects of cybersecurity, providing comprehensive insights to empower users in their journey toward a secure and confident digital existence. Let the knowledge gained here be the shield that guards your digital realm, ensuring that your online experiences remain safe and secure in the face of evolving cyber threats.

Chapter 5: Eyes in the Sky - Surveillance and Privacy Protection

In the interconnected landscape of the digital age, concerns about surveillance and privacy have become increasingly prevalent. This chapter delves into the intricate web of digital surveillance, providing insights and strategies to empower average home users in safeguarding their privacy against prying eyes. Understanding the surveillance methods, implementing privacy protection measures, and navigating the delicate balance between convenience and security is crucial for individuals seeking control over their digital lives.

5.1 The Pervasiveness of Digital Surveillance

Digital surveillance has woven itself into the fabric of our online interactions, manifesting in various forms across different platforms and technologies. Understanding the extent of surveillance is the first step toward reclaiming control over personal data.

- Internet Service Providers (ISPs): ISPs can monitor users' internet activities, including websites visited, search queries, and even the content of unencrypted communications.
- Social Media Platforms: Social media platforms collect vast user data, tracking preferences, interactions, and offline activities through integrated features and third-party applications.
- Online Advertisers and Trackers: Advertisers employ tracking technologies to monitor users' online behavior, creating detailed profiles for targeted advertising; this extends beyond websites and includes mobile apps.
- Government Surveillance: Governments may engage in surveillance for national security purposes, monitoring communications, online activities, and even physical movements through various means.

5.2 Risks and Implications of Digital Surveillance

The implications of digital surveillance extend beyond data collection, encompassing potential risks that can impact individual privacy and security.

- Identity Theft: Aggregating personal information increases the risk of identity theft, where malicious actors exploit stolen data for fraudulent activities.
- Targeted Advertising: Extensive profiling enables targeted advertising, which, while ostensibly personalized, can lead to the manipulation of consumer behavior and preferences.
- Data Breaches: Surveillance data, when inadequately protected, becomes a valuable target for cybercriminals, leading to large-scale data breaches with severe consequences for individuals.
- Government Intrusion: Government surveillance raises concerns about privacy, civil liberties, and potential abuse.

5.3 Understanding Privacy Policies and Terms of Service

Before diving into privacy protection measures, users must comprehend the privacy policies and terms of service associated with their platforms and services. These documents outline how user data is collected, stored, and shared.

- Readability and Transparency: Seek platforms and services with transparent and easily understandable privacy policies. Avoid convoluted or ambiguous language that may obscure the true extent of data collection.
- Data Sharing Practices: Examine how platforms share user data with third parties. Be cautious of services that engage in extensive data sharing without explicit user consent.
- Retention Periods: Understand how long platforms retain user data. Some services may keep data indefinitely, while others have established retention periods.

5.4 Privacy Protection Measures for Internet Browsing

Browsing the internet is a primary avenue for data collection. Still, there are practical measures to enhance privacy without sacrificing the convenience of online activities.

- Use of Virtual Private Networks (VPNs): VPNs encrypt internet traffic, obscuring it from ISPs and potential eavesdroppers; this helps maintain anonymity and protects against data interception.
- Browser Privacy Settings: Modern browsers offer privacy settings that allow users to control cookie tracking, block third-party cookies, and enable "Do Not Track" requests.
- Search Engine Privacy: Consider using privacy-focused search engines that don't track user searches or store personal information.

5.5 Social Media Privacy Settings and Practices

As hubs of personal information, social media platforms require careful management of privacy settings to control the visibility of user data.

- Profile Privacy Settings: Adjust profile privacy settings to restrict the visibility of personal information to a select audience—limit who can view posts, friend lists, and other profile details.
- Third-Party App Permissions: Regularly review and manage permissions granted to third-party apps connected to social media accounts. Remove access for apps that are no longer used or deemed unnecessary.
- Post Visibility Controls: Utilize post visibility controls to tailor the audience for each post; this ensures that sensitive information is shared only with the intended audience.

5.6 Email Encryption and Secure Communication

Email, a commonly used communication tool, can be vulnerable to interception. Encrypting emails and adopting secure communication practices mitigate these risks.

- End-to-end Encryption: Use email services that offer end-to-end encryption, ensuring that only the intended recipient can decipher the contents of the email.
- Secure Messaging Apps: For real-time communication, consider using certain messaging apps that prioritize encryption, protecting the confidentiality of conversations.

5.7 Password Protection and Two-Factor Authentication (2FA)

The importance of robust password protection and adopting two-factor authentication (2FA) cannot be overstated in the context of privacy defense.

- Solid and Unique Passwords: Maintain strong and unique passwords for all accounts. Avoid using easily guessable information and employ a password manager for enhanced security.
- Two-Factor Authentication: Enable 2FA whenever possible. This additional layer of security prevents unauthorized access even if passwords are compromised.

5.8 Privacy-Focused Operating Systems and Tools

Privacy concerns do not stop at individual practices; the choice of operating systems and digital tools can significantly impact overall privacy.
- Privacy-Focused Browsers: Explore browsers designed with privacy in mind, such as Firefox, which has enhanced privacy features, or privacy-focused alternatives like Brave or DuckDuckGo.

- Operating Systems: Some operating systems, like Linux distributions and privacy-focused mobile operating systems, prioritize user privacy and security.

5.9 IoT Devices and Home Network Security

As the Internet of Things (IoT) proliferates, securing IoT devices and home networks is essential for preventing unauthorized surveillance and data breaches.

- Change Default Passwords: Many IoT devices come with default passwords. Change these passwords immediately to prevent unauthorized access.
- Network Encryption: Secure your home network with encryption (e.g., WPA3 for Wi-Fi) to prevent unauthorized access to connected devices.
- Regular Firmware Updates: Keep IoT device firmware updated to patch vulnerabilities and improve overall security.

5.10 Privacy-Conscious App Usage

The apps installed on devices can be conduits for data collection. Adopting privacy-conscious practices when using apps is crucial.

- App Permissions: Review and manage app permissions regularly. Disable unnecessary permissions that grant access to sensitive data.
- Limit Location Tracking: Restrict location tracking for apps that don't require it for essential functionality. Consider using "location only while using the app" settings.
- Regular App Audits: Periodically review installed apps and uninstall those no longer needed; this reduces the potential for data exposure through unused or forgotten apps.

5.11 VPNs for Enhanced Privacy

Virtual Private Networks (VPNs) are powerful tools for safeguarding privacy by encrypting internet traffic and masking the user's IP address.

- Choosing a Reputable VPN Service: Select a reputable VPN service that prioritizes user privacy, with a no-logs policy and robust encryption protocols.
- Usage of Public Wi-Fi: Utilize VPNs when connecting to public Wi-Fi networks to secure communications and prevent potential eavesdropping.
- Understanding VPN Limitations: VPNs enhance privacy but are not a one-size-fits-all solution. Users should be aware of the limitations and choose complementary privacy protection measures.

5.12 Privacy Education for Children and Family Members

Promoting privacy awareness within the family is crucial, especially considering the increased digital presence of children.

- Educational Initiatives: Introduce educational programs or games that teach children about online privacy, safe internet usage, and the potential risks associated with oversharing.
- Parental Controls: Implement parental control features on devices used by children, ensuring a safe digital environment and limiting exposure to age-inappropriate content.
- Open Communication: Foster open communication within the family about privacy concerns and the importance of responsible digital behavior.

5.13 Dealing with Surveillance Cameras and Smart Home Devices

Integrating surveillance cameras and smart home devices into daily life raises privacy concerns. Understanding and managing these devices is essential.

- Review Default Settings: Upon acquiring surveillance cameras or smart home devices, review and adjust default settings to align with privacy preferences.
- Disable Unnecessary Features: Disable any features or functionalities that are not essential. For example, turn off audio recording on smart home devices if unnecessary.
- Regular Device Audits: Periodically audit connected devices for unauthorized access, software vulnerabilities, or potential security risks.

5.14 Legal Considerations and Privacy Advocacy

Understanding legal frameworks and advocating for privacy rights contribute to a comprehensive approach to digital privacy.

- Know Your Rights: Familiarize yourself with privacy laws and regulations applicable to your region. Understand your rights concerning data protection and privacy.
- Support Privacy Advocacy Groups: Contribute to or support organizations advocating digital privacy rights. Stay informed about initiatives working to protect user privacy on a broader scale.

5.15 Conclusion: Navigating the Privacy Landscape

As we navigate the digital landscape, the balance between convenience and privacy becomes paramount. Empowered with knowledge and armed with privacy protection measures, average home users can assert control over their digital lives. The measures discussed in this chapter serve as a guide, allowing individuals to be more discerning in their online activities and mindful of the digital footprints they leave behind.

In the forthcoming chapters, we will continue exploring cybersecurity facets that empower users to navigate the ever-evolving digital realm confidently. May the knowledge gained here be a beacon, guiding you through the complexities of digital privacy and ensuring that your online experiences are secure, private, and under your control.

Chapter 6: Safe Harbors - Securing Your Online Transactions

Securing financial interactions in the virtual realm is paramount in an era where digital transactions have become integral to our daily lives. This chapter explores the nuances of online transactions, offering insights and strategies to empower average home users in safeguarding their financial well-being. From secure payment methods to recognizing potential threats, understanding the landscape of online transactions is crucial for confidently navigating the digital economic frontier.

6.1 The Evolution of Digital Transactions

The landscape of financial transactions has undergone a revolutionary shift with the advent of digital technology. From the early days of online shopping to the widespread adoption of mobile payment apps, the convenience of digital transactions has become synonymous with modern living.

- E-commerce Boom: The rise of e-commerce platforms has transformed how we shop, enabling users to browse and purchase various products from the comfort of their homes.
- Mobile Payments: The ubiquity of smartphones has given rise to mobile payment apps, allowing users to make transactions, pay bills, and transfer funds with a few taps on their devices.
- Cryptocurrencies: The emergence of cryptocurrencies, led by Bitcoin and others, has introduced decentralized digital currencies that operate on blockchain technology.

6.2 The Importance of Secure Online Transactions

While the convenience of digital transactions is undeniable, the potential risks associated with online financial activities require vigilant safeguards. Understanding the importance of secure online transactions is the first step in fortifying the digital wallet.

- Financial Data Sensitivity: Digital transactions often involve exchanging sensitive financial information, including credit card details, bank account numbers, and personal identifiers. Protecting this information is crucial to prevent unauthorized access and fraud.

- Identity Theft Risks: Cybercriminals actively target financial data for identity theft, using stolen information to commit fraudulent activities, open accounts, or make unauthorized purchases.
- Transaction Security: Ensuring the security of transactions is vital for preventing interception, tampering, or unauthorized access while exchanging funds.

6.3 Secure Payment Methods: Choosing Your Digital Armor

Selecting secure payment methods is akin to choosing armor for digital financial transactions. Various options offer different levels of protection, and users must weigh factors such as convenience, accessibility, and security.

- Credit and Debit Cards: Widely used for online transactions, credit and debit cards offer convenience and buyer protection features. Users should regularly monitor transactions and report any unauthorized activity promptly.
- Digital Wallets: Mobile payment apps and digital wallets, such as Apple Pay, Google Pay, and Samsung Pay, provide security through tokenization and biometric authentication.
- Cryptocurrencies: Cryptocurrencies, like Bitcoin and Ethereum, offer a decentralized and pseudonymous means of conducting transactions. While providing a degree of privacy, users must be mindful of crypto's volatility and security considerations.
- Secure Online Banking: Utilizing specific online banking platforms allows users to manage and monitor their accounts, set up transaction alerts, and employ two-factor authentication for added security.

6.4 Recognizing and Avoiding Phishing Threats

Phishing threats pose a significant risk to the security of online transactions. Cybercriminals employ deceptive tactics to trick users into revealing sensitive information. Recognizing and avoiding phishing attempts is crucial for maintaining a secure online financial environment.

- Email Phishing: Be cautious of unsolicited emails that request sensitive information or contain links to seemingly legitimate websites. Verify the legitimacy of emails before clicking on links or providing any information.
- Website Verification: Verify its legitimacy before entering payment information on a website. Check for secure connections (https://), look for trust seals, and ensure the website's URL is spelled correctly.
- Two-Factor Authentication (2FA): Enable 2FA whenever possible, especially for online banking and payment platforms. This additional layer of security mitigates the risk of unauthorized access, even if login credentials are compromised.

6.5 Secure Wi-Fi Practices for Financial Transactions

The security of Wi-Fi networks directly impacts the safety of online transactions conducted over these networks. Implementing secure Wi-Fi practices is essential for preventing unauthorized access and data interception.

- Password Protection: Secure your Wi-Fi network with a robust and unique password. Avoid using default passwords and regularly update them to prevent unauthorized access.
- Wi-Fi Encryption: Utilize robust encryption protocols, such as WPA3, to encrypt data transmitted over the Wi-Fi network; this prevents eavesdropping and unauthorized access to sensitive information.
- Guest Network Usage: Create a separate guest network for visitors; this segregates guest traffic from the leading network, enhancing overall security.

6.6 Best Practices for Online Transaction Security

In addition to selecting secure payment methods and recognizing potential threats, adopting best practices for online transaction security contributes to a robust defense against financial fraud.

- Regularly Monitor Transactions: Review and monitor financial transactions for unauthorized or suspicious activity. Promptly report any discrepancies to the relevant financial institution.
- Update Software and Apps: Keep devices, operating systems, and financial apps updated with the latest security patches. Software updates often include fixes for vulnerabilities that cybercriminals could exploit.
- Use Dedicated Devices: Use dedicated devices for online financial transactions whenever possible. Avoid conducting sensitive transactions on public computers or shared devices.

6.7 Privacy and Security Settings on E-commerce Platforms

E-commerce platforms play a central role in online shopping, and users can enhance transaction security by leveraging the privacy and security features offered by these platforms.

- Account Security Settings: Strengthen account security by enabling two-factor authentication, updating passwords regularly, and reviewing connected devices.
- Payment Methods: Regularly review and update saved payment methods. Remove outdated or unused payment information to reduce the risk of unauthorized transactions.
- Transaction History: Review transaction history on e-commerce platforms to ensure all transactions are legitimate. Report any unauthorized purchases promptly.

6.8 Mobile Payment Security Considerations

With the prevalence of mobile payment apps, users must be aware of security considerations specific to these platforms.

- Biometric Authentication: Enable biometric authentication for mobile payment apps, such as fingerprint or facial recognition; this adds an extra layer of security beyond PIN codes or passwords.
- Lost or Stolen Devices: Report lost or stolen devices to the relevant financial institutions immediately. Many mobile payment apps offer features to lock or wipe the device to prevent unauthorized remote access.
- Secure App Downloads: Only download mobile payment apps from official app stores to ensure the authenticity and security of the application.

6.9 Safe Online Investment Practices

Adopting safe practices is crucial for those engaging in online investments or trading to protect financial assets and sensitive information.

- Use Reputable Platforms: Choose reputable investment platforms prioritizing security and employing encryption protocols to safeguard user data.
- Enable Two-Factor Authentication: Enhance the security of investment accounts by enabling two-factor authentication, which protects against unauthorized access.
- Regularly Review Investments: Periodically review investment portfolios and transaction history. Report any suspicious activity promptly to the investment platform.

6.10 Fraud Reporting and Resolution

In the unfortunate event of falling victim to financial fraud or unauthorized transactions, knowing the steps for fraud reporting and resolution is crucial.

- Contact Financial Institution: Contact the relevant financial institution immediately to report the unauthorized transaction. Many institutions have dedicated fraud reporting hotlines for expedited assistance.
- File a Police Report: In cases of identity theft or severe fraud, filing a police report provides a legal record of the incident and can aid in the resolution process.
- Credit Reporting Agencies: Report the incident to credit reporting agencies to place fraud alerts on your credit reports, preventing further unauthorized activities.

6.11 The Future of Secure Transactions: Emerging Technologies

As technology evolves, so do the methods and technologies to secure online transactions. Emerging technologies promise to enhance the security of digital financial interactions further.

- Biometric Authentication Advances: Continued advancements in biometric authentication, such as palm vein recognition and behavioral biometrics, offer more secure and convenient ways to verify identities.
- Blockchain and Decentralized Finance (DeFi): Using blockchain technology and decentralized finance (DeFi) can revolutionize financial transactions by providing transparent, secure, and decentralized platforms.
- Quantum-Safe Cryptography: With the rise of quantum computing, the development and adoption of quantum-safe cryptography have become imperative to ensure the continued security of online transactions.

6.12 Conclusion: Navigating the Digital Financial Seas

As we navigate the digital financial seas, securing online transactions becomes a foundational element of a confident and resilient digital existence. This chapter's strategies and insights aim to empower average home users to make informed choices, recognize potential threats, and adopt practices that fortify their financial well-being in the digital realm.

In the forthcoming chapters, we will continue our exploration of cybersecurity, delving into topics that empower users to navigate the ever-evolving digital landscape with knowledge and assurance. May the information provided here serve as a compass, guiding you through the complexities of online transactions and ensuring that your digital financial voyage remains safe, secure, and under your control.

Chapter 7: The Trojan Horse - Social Engineering and Phishing

In the vast cybersecurity landscape, where technology is both a shield and a vulnerability, the human factor remains a critical focal point. This chapter explores the insidious tactics of social engineering and phishing, unveiling the art of manipulation that cybercriminals employ to exploit human trust. As average home users, understanding these tactics is crucial for building a resilient defense against the deceptive Trojan horses that lurk in the digital shadows.

7.1 Unmasking the Trojan Horse: Social Engineering Defined

At the heart of many cyber threats lies a human touch, a psychological manipulation known as "social engineering" that preys on trust, curiosity, or fear. Social engineering involves exploiting human psychology to access sensitive information, often leading to unauthorized access, fraud, or other malicious activities.

- Trust Exploitation: Cybercriminals leverage trust to trick individuals into divulging confidential information; this could be through impersonation, where the attacker poses as a trustworthy entity.
- Manipulating Emotions: Emotional manipulation is a common tactic, exploiting emotions such as fear, urgency, or excitement to prompt impulsive actions from the victim.
- Information Gathering: Social engineers often collect information from various sources to create convincing scenarios or personas, using the information to tailor their approach and make the deception more believable.

7.2 The Art of Deception: Common Social Engineering Techniques
Social engineering comes in various forms, each tailored to exploit specific aspects of human behavior. Understanding these techniques is crucial for averting potential threats.

- Phishing: Phishing involves sending deceptive messages, often masquerading as legitimate entities, to trick recipients into revealing sensitive information, such as login credentials or financial details.
- Pretexting: In pretexting, attackers create a fabricated scenario to gain the target's trust; this could involve impersonating a colleague, tech support personnel, or a trusted service provider.
- Baiting: Baiting involves enticing individuals with promises of something desirable, such as free software or media, to trick them into downloading malicious content.
- Quizzes and Surveys: Cybercriminals may use seemingly innocent quizzes or surveys to gather personal information. These seemingly harmless activities can lead to data compromise.

7.3 The Phishing Expedition: Understanding and Defending Against Phishing Attacks
Among the various social engineering techniques, phishing is among the most prevalent and influential. Recognizing phishing attempts and adopting preventive measures are vital for averting potential risks.

- Email Phishing: Be cautious of unsolicited emails, especially those urging urgent action or requesting sensitive information. Verify the legitimacy of the sender and avoid clicking on suspicious links.
- Website Verification: Always verify the legitimacy of websites, primarily when directed there through email links. Check for secure connections (https://) and ensure the website's URL is spelled correctly.

- Avoiding Email Attachments: Exercise caution when opening email attachments, even if they appear to come from a known contact. Attachments can contain malware or lead to phishing websites.
- Two-Factor Authentication (2FA): Enable 2FA for email accounts and other online services. Even if login credentials are compromised, 2FA adds a layer of protection.

7.4 Recognizing Pretexting and Building Defense Mechanisms

Pretexting involves creating a fabricated scenario to manipulate individuals into divulging sensitive information. Recognizing and defending against pretexting requires a heightened awareness of potential red flags.

- Verify Identity: When in doubt, verify the identity of the person or entity making a request. Use trusted channels, such as official contact information, to confirm the request's legitimacy.
- Question Unusual Requests: Be skeptical of unusual or unexpected requests, susceptible information, or financial transactions. Confirm the request through established channels.
- Limit Personal Information Sharing: Minimize sharing personal information, especially over the phone or through non-secure communication channels. Be cautious of requests for information that seems unnecessary.

7.5 Baiting: Resisting the Temptation of the Digital Lure

Baiting tactics often involve offering something enticing to lure individuals into compromising situations. Building resilience against baiting requires a combination of skepticism and proactive measures.

- Avoiding Unknown Downloads: Refrain from downloading files or clicking on links from unknown or untrusted sources. Verify the legitimacy of offers or downloads before taking any action.
- Secure File Sharing: Use specific file-sharing platforms for legitimate downloads. Be cautious of downloading files from unsecured or suspicious websites.
- Educational Initiatives: Educate yourself and others about the risks of baiting tactics. Awareness is a powerful defense against falling victim to deceptive offers.

7.6 Protecting Against Quizzes and Surveys: Guarding Your Data

Quizzes and surveys, seemingly harmless and entertaining, can be avenues for social engineers to collect personal information. Implementing protective measures ensures that your data remains secure.
- Limit Participation: Be selective in participating in online quizzes and surveys. Avoid providing unnecessary personal information, especially if the source is unfamiliar.

- Check Privacy Settings: Review and adjust privacy settings on social media platforms to limit the availability of personal information to external parties.
- Verify Source Credibility: Verify the source's credibility before participating in a quiz or survey. Legitimate surveys are typically associated with reputable organizations or platforms.

7.7 Social Engineering in the Age of Social Media

The prevalence of social media platforms has created new avenues for social engineers to gather information and manipulate individuals. Mitigating these risks involves a combination of cautious behavior and privacy management.

- Review Privacy Settings: Regularly review and update privacy settings on social media platforms. Restrict the visibility of personal information to a limited audience.
- Be Mindful of Connections: Be cautious when accepting friend requests or connections from unknown individuals. Cybercriminals may use fake profiles to gather information.
- Think Before Sharing: Consider the potential implications before sharing personal information or updates. Bad actors can use information shared on social media for pretexting or targeted phishing attacks.

7.8 Social Engineering in Email Communications: Defending Your Inbox

Email remains a primary communication channel, making it a common target for social engineering attacks. Strengthening your email defense involves a combination of technology and user awareness.

- Email Filtering: Use filtering tools to identify and filter out phishing emails. These tools analyze incoming emails for known patterns and characteristics associated with phishing.
- Be Skeptical of Unsolicited Emails: Exercise caution when receiving unsolicited emails, especially those urging urgent action or requesting sensitive information. Verify the legitimacy of the sender before taking any action.
- Hover Over Links: Before clicking on any email links, hover over them to preview the URL. Be cautious of mismatched or suspicious URLs that may lead to phishing websites.

7.9 Building a Human Firewall: Cybersecurity Education

Empowering individuals to become a robust line of defense against social engineering involves ongoing cybersecurity education. Awareness programs and training initiatives contribute to the development of a human firewall.

- Security Awareness Training: Engage in security awareness training programs that cover the tactics and techniques employed by social engineers. Understand common red flags and how to respond.

- Regular Updates on Threat Landscape: Stay informed about the evolving threat landscape. Cybersecurity threats, including social engineering tactics, are dynamic, and regular updates help individuals adapt to new challenges.
- Phishing Simulations: Participate in phishing simulations conducted by organizations or security experts. These simulations provide hands-on experience in recognizing and avoiding phishing attempts.

7.10 Reporting Incidents and Seeking Assistance

Despite preventive measures, incidents may still occur. Promptly reporting suspicious activity and seeking assistance is crucial for mitigating potential risks.

- Internal Reporting Procedures: Organizations often have internal reporting procedures for suspicious activity. Familiarize yourself with these procedures and report any incidents promptly.
- Cybersecurity Helplines: Many countries have cybersecurity helplines that individuals can contact for guidance and assistance. Report incidents and seek advice from these helplines.
- Professional Assistance: In cases of severe social engineering attacks or data breaches, seeking professional cybersecurity assistance may be necessary. Cybersecurity experts can guide incident response and recovery.

7.11 The Role of Technology in Social Engineering Defense

While human awareness is critical to social engineering defense, technology complements cybersecurity measures.

- Advanced Threat Protection: Implement advanced threat protection solutions that utilize artificial intelligence and machine learning to identify and block sophisticated social engineering attacks.
- Email Authentication Protocols: Utilize email authentication protocols, such as SPF, DKIM, and DMARC, to verify the authenticity of incoming emails. These protocols help prevent email spoofing and phishing attempts.
- Multi-Layered Security: Deploy a multi-layered security approach that includes firewalls, antivirus software, and intrusion detection systems. This layered defense helps detect and block various types of social engineering attacks.

7.12 The Future of Social Engineering Defense: Technological Innovations

As technology evolves, so do the tools and innovations available for defending against social engineering attacks. Emerging technologies hold promise in enhancing the overall resilience of individuals and organizations.

- Behavioral Biometrics: Integrating behavioral biometrics, such as typing patterns and mouse movements, adds a layer of authentication by recognizing unique user behaviors.
- Artificial Intelligence (AI) in Threat Detection: AI-driven threat detection systems continue to evolve, offering real-time analysis of user behavior and communication patterns to identify potential social engineering attacks.
- Blockchain for Identity Verification: Blockchain technology has the potential to revolutionize identity verification, providing a decentralized and tamper-resistant method for confirming the legitimacy of entities.

7.13 Conclusion: Fortifying the Human Element

In the perpetual cat-and-mouse game between cybercriminals and cybersecurity defenders, the human element remains both the target and the defense. As average home users, the knowledge gained in this chapter equips you with the tools to recognize the Trojan horses of social engineering and phishing.

May the insights shared here be a beacon, guiding you through the intricacies of digital manipulation and fortifying your defenses against the deceptive tactics employed by cyber adversaries. In the upcoming chapters, we will continue our journey through cybersecurity, exploring topics that empower you to navigate the digital landscape with resilience and confidence.

Chapter 8: Firewalls and Moats - Advanced Network Defense

In the ever-expanding digital landscape, your home network serves as the fortress protecting your digital kingdom. This chapter delves into advanced network defense, exploring the crucial role of firewalls and other protective measures. As an average home user, understanding how to fortify your digital moat is essential for securing your online presence and thwarting potential cyber threats.

8.1 The Digital Moat: Understanding Home Networks

Your home network is the cornerstone of your digital defense. Imagine it as a moat surrounding your castle, providing a barrier between your devices and the vast, sometimes treacherous, digital wilderness. Understanding the components of this digital moat is the first step in building a robust defense.

- Router as the Gateway Guardian: The router, acting as the gateway to the internet, is your first line of defense. It directs traffic between your devices and the internet, making it a crucial component of network security.
- Devices as Soldiers: Each device connected to your network, from smartphones to laptops and smart appliances, is a soldier defending your digital realm. However, these soldiers can be protected with proper coordination and defense strategies.
- The Crown Jewels: The data flowing through your network is the crown jewel of your digital kingdom. From personal documents to sensitive financial information, safeguarding this data is paramount.

8.2 The Guardian at the Gate: The Role of Firewalls

At the heart of your digital moat is the guardian at the gate – the firewall. A firewall acts as a barrier between your internal network and the external world, monitoring and controlling incoming and outgoing network traffic based on predetermined security rules. Understanding the different types of firewalls is essential for effective network defense.

- Hardware Firewalls: Typically integrated into routers, hardware firewalls filter traffic at the router level before it reaches your devices. They are the first line of defense against external threats.
- Software Firewalls: Software firewalls provide an additional layer of protection by monitoring and controlling traffic specific to that device. They are handy for laptops and desktop computers.
- Unified Threat Management (UTM) Devices: UTM devices combine multiple security features, including firewalls, intrusion detection, and antivirus capabilities. These all-in-one solutions provide comprehensive protection for your network.

8.3 Fortifying the Moat: Configuring Your Firewall

Configuring your firewall effectively is akin to fortifying the walls of your castle. Understanding the settings and features of your firewall allows you to tailor its defense mechanisms to your specific needs.

- Default Deny Rule: Adopt a default deny rule, allowing only necessary traffic and blocking all incoming and outgoing connections. This principle ensures that only approved communication is permitted.
- Port and Protocol Management: Control which ports and protocols are open on your firewall. Closing unnecessary ports reduces the potential entry points for cyber threats.

- Application Filtering: Utilize application filtering features to control the types of applications that can access the internet; this helps prevent malicious software or unauthorized applications from communicating externally.
- Intrusion Prevention Systems (IPS): Activate IPS features to detect and block suspicious activities or known attack patterns. IPS adds an extra layer of defense against sophisticated cyber threats.

8.4 The Watchtower: Intrusion Detection Systems (IDS)

While firewalls act as the primary gatekeepers, intrusion detection systems (IDS) serve as watchtowers, actively monitoring network traffic for signs of suspicious activity or potential security breaches.

- Signature-Based Detection: IDS systems often use signature-based detection, comparing network traffic patterns against a database of known attack signatures. The system triggers an alert if a match is found.
- Behavioral-Based Detection: Some IDS solutions use behavioral-based detection to analyze deviations from normal network behavior. This approach is practical against previously unknown or zero-day attacks.
- Network and Host-Based IDS: Network-based IDS monitors overall network traffic, while host-based IDS focuses on the activities of individual devices. Implementing both provides a comprehensive defense strategy.

8.5 The Sentinel: Antivirus and Anti-malware Defenses

Malware lurks like hidden assailants waiting to breach your defenses in the digital wilderness. Antivirus and anti-malware defenses act as sentinels, scanning for and neutralizing these threats.

- Real-Time Scanning: Enable real-time scanning features to detect and remove malware as soon as it attempts to infiltrate your system. This proactive approach prevents malicious software from causing harm.
- Regular Updates: Keep antivirus and anti-malware databases updated to ensure they can recognize the latest threats. Cybercriminals continually evolve their tactics, and regular updates are essential for staying ahead.
- Scheduled Scans: Implement scans to examine your system for potential threats thoroughly. Regular scans help identify and remove dormant or hidden malware.

8.6 Virtual Private Networks (VPNs): Stealth in the Digital Shadows

In the digital realm, prying eyes can intercept and observe your data. Virtual Private Networks (VPNs) act as stealth cloaks, encrypting your internet connection and protecting your data from potential eavesdroppers.

- Secure Data Encryption: VPNs encrypt your internet connection, making it difficult for third parties to intercept and decipher the data transmitted between your device and the internet.
- Anonymized IP Addresses: VPNs mask your IP address, adding an extra layer of anonymity to your online activities; this helps protect your privacy and prevents tracking by websites and malicious actors.
- Public Wi-Fi Security: VPNs ensure a secure and encrypted connection when connected to public Wi-Fi networks, reducing the risk of unauthorized access and data interception.

8.7 Network Segmentation: Dividing and Conquering Threats

A castle is not a single entity but a collection of strategically segmented areas. Similarly, network segmentation involves dividing your network into isolated segments, limiting the impact of potential security breaches.

- Guest Networks: Create separate guest networks to isolate guest devices from your primary network; this prevents potential threats from spreading to other devices.
- IoT Device Segmentation: Internet of Things (IoT) devices often have varying security levels. Segmenting IoT devices from critical devices enhances network security by containing potential vulnerabilities.
- User and Admin Segmentation: Implement user and administrative segmentation to restrict access to critical network resources; this ensures that only authorized individuals can access sensitive data or configurations.

8.8 Continuous Monitoring and Threat Intelligence

In the world of digital defense, vigilance is paramount. Continuous monitoring of your network, coupled with access to threat intelligence, provides an ongoing awareness of potential risks.

- Network Traffic Analysis: Utilize network traffic analysis tools to monitor ongoing activities and identify anomalies. This proactive approach allows for the early detection of potential threats.
- Threat Intelligence Feeds: Subscribe to threat intelligence feeds that provide real-time information about emerging cyber threats. Staying informed about the latest tactics and vulnerabilities enhances your ability to defend against potential attacks preemptively.

- Security Information and Event Management (SIEM): Implement SIEM solutions that aggregate and analyze log data from various network components. SIEM tools provide a comprehensive view of network activities, aiding in detecting potential security incidents.

8.9 Securing Wireless Networks: Locking the Castle Gates

Wireless networks are susceptible to unauthorized access if not properly secured. Implementing robust security measures for your Wi-Fi network is essential for preventing unwanted intruders.

- Robust Encryption Protocols: Utilize strong encryption protocols, such as WPA3, to secure your Wi-Fi network; this prevents unauthorized access and ensures that data transmitted over the network is encrypted.
- Unique and Strong Passwords: Set unique and strong passwords for your Wi-Fi network. Avoid using default passwords, as these are easily exploited by attackers attempting to gain access.
- Wi-Fi Network Name (SSID) Hiding: Consider hiding the SSID of your Wi-Fi network to make it less visible to potential attackers. While not foolproof, this adds an extra layer of obscurity.

8.10 The Human Element in Network Defense: User Education

Even with advanced technological defenses, the human element remains a crucial factor. Educating yourself and other users in your household enhances overall network security.

- Phishing Awareness: Train users to recognize phishing attempts and avoid clicking on suspicious links or providing sensitive information in response to unsolicited emails.
- Device Hygiene Practices: Promote good device hygiene practices, such as regularly updating software and applications, to patch vulnerabilities and prevent exploitation by attackers.
- Password Management: Encourage the use of strong, unique passwords for each device and online account. Implement password management tools to simplify creating and managing secure passwords.

8.11 The Future of Network Defense: Evolving Technologies

As technology evolves, so do the tools and technologies available for network defense. Emerging innovations hold promise in enhancing the security of home networks against ever-evolving cyber threats.

- Artificial Intelligence (AI) in Network Security: AI-driven network security solutions analyze vast amounts of data to identify patterns and anomalies, enabling proactive threat detection and response.

- Zero Trust Architecture: Zero Trust involves treating every user and device as untrusted, regardless of their location within the network. This approach minimizes the risk of lateral movement by attackers.
- Software-Defined Networking (SDN): SDN enables dynamic network configuration and management, allowing for swift response to security incidents and changes in network traffic patterns.

8.12 Conclusion: Fortifying Your Digital Citadel

In the intricate dance between cybersecurity threats and defense, your home network is the digital citadel protecting your digital kingdom. The strategies and insights shared in this chapter are designed to empower average home users in fortifying their digital moats against potential cyber threats.

As we venture further into cybersecurity, each chapter serves as a guidepost, equipping you with the knowledge and tools to navigate the ever-evolving digital landscape. In the chapters ahead, we will continue exploring topics that empower you to wield your digital defenses with confidence and resilience.

Chapter 9: Lock and Key - Encryption in Everyday Life

In the vast expanse of the digital world, where information travels at the speed of light, ensuring the privacy and security of your data is paramount. This chapter explores the fundamental concept of encryption, a digital lock and key mechanism that safeguards your digital communications and sensitive information. As an average home user, understanding how encryption works and where it plays a role in your everyday life empowers you to navigate the digital landscape with confidence and privacy.

9.1 The Essence of Encryption: A Digital Lock and Key

At its core, encryption transforms information into an unreadable format, often called ciphertext, using a cryptographic algorithm and a key. This process ensures that only individuals with the corresponding key can decrypt and access the original information. Imagine it as a lock and key mechanism, where your data is the valuable content secured within a digital vault.

- Cryptography Unveiled: Cryptography, the science behind encryption, encompasses a range of mathematical techniques and algorithms designed to secure communication and data. It provides the foundation for the creation of secure digital locks.

- Keys as Access Codes: In the encryption metaphor, keys act as digital access codes. The encryption key transforms the original information into ciphertext, and the decryption key is required to revert the ciphertext to its original form.
- Public and Private Keys: Public-key cryptography involves using a pair of keys: a public key, which is shared openly, and a private key, which is kept secret. The public key encrypts information, and only the corresponding private key can decrypt it.

9.2 Everyday Encounters: Where Encryption Lurks

Encryption is not an esoteric concept reserved for the digital elite; it permeates many aspects of your daily interactions with technology. Recognizing these scenarios sheds light on the ubiquity and importance of encryption in safeguarding your digital life.

- Secure Websites and HTTPS: When you browse the internet, especially when handling sensitive information like passwords or credit card details, you often encounter websites with addresses starting with "https://" instead of "http://." The "s" stands for secure, indicating the connection is encrypted.
- Messaging Apps and End-to-End Encryption: Popular messaging applications like WhatsApp and Signal implement end-to-end encryption; only the sender and intended recipient can decrypt and read the messages, ensuring privacy even if the communication passes through servers.
- Online Banking Transactions: When conducting online banking transactions or accessing your financial accounts, encryption safeguards your sensitive financial data. The padlock icon in the address bar signifies a secure, encrypted connection.
- Email Encryption: Some email services offer encryption options, allowing you to send encrypted emails; this ensures that the content of your messages remains private and secure from unauthorized access.

9.3 The Encryption Arms Race: Understanding Symmetric and Asymmetric Encryption

There are two primary approaches in the realm of encryption: symmetric and asymmetric. Each method has its strengths and uses, contributing to the intricate tapestry of digital security.

- Symmetric Encryption: A single key is used for encryption and decryption in symmetric encryption. The challenge lies in securely sharing this key between parties. While efficient, it requires a secure initial key exchange.
- Asymmetric Encryption: Asymmetric encryption employs a pair of keys: a public key for encryption and a private key for decryption; this eliminates the need for a shared key, enhancing security. Public-key cryptography is a prominent example of asymmetric encryption.

9.4 TLS/SSL Protocols: Safeguarding Your Online Transactions

Transport Layer Security (TLS) and its predecessor, Secure Sockets Layer (SSL), are cryptographic protocols that secure communication over a computer network. These protocols play a vital role in ensuring the security of your online interactions, particularly when transmitting sensitive information.

- Establishing Secure Connections: When you visit a secure website, TLS or SSL protocols establish an encrypted connection between your browser and the website's server; this prevents third parties from intercepting or tampering with the data exchanged.
- Authentication and Integrity: TLS and SSL provide mechanisms for server authentication, ensuring that you connect to the intended website. Additionally, they maintain data integrity, preventing unauthorized modification during transmission.
- Evolution of Protocols: Over time, TLS and SSL protocols evolve to address vulnerabilities and enhance security. It is essential to use up-to-date protocols to benefit from the latest cryptographic advancements and security features.

9.5 The Digital Vault: Full Disk Encryption and File Encryption

Beyond securing your online interactions, encryption extends its protective shield to the physical devices you use daily. Full disk and file encryption are the digital vaults safeguarding your data.

- Full Disk Encryption: Full disk encryption ensures that all data on your computer's storage drive is encrypted; this protects your files and information, even if your device falls into the wrong hands.
- File Encryption: File encryption lets you selectively encrypt specific files or folders; this is particularly useful for securing sensitive documents, such as financial records or personal journals, on a shared device.
- BitLocker, FileVault, and VeraCrypt: Operating systems often include built-in encryption tools like BitLocker for Windows, FileVault for macOS, and third-party solutions like VeraCrypt. These tools facilitate the implementation of full disk and file-level encryption.

9.6 Virtual Private Networks (VPNs): Encryption on the Virtual Highway

Virtual Private Networks (VPNs), commonly known for ensuring anonymity, also play a pivotal role in encryption. They establish secure tunnels, encrypting your internet connection and shielding your online activities from prying eyes.

- Tunneling and Encryption: VPNs use tunneling protocols to create a secure pathway between your device and the VPN server. Within this tunnel, data is encrypted, preventing eavesdroppers from deciphering the transmitted information.

- Anonymity and Privacy: While encryption is a core feature of VPNs, these services enhance online privacy by masking your IP address; this prevents websites and online services from tracking your digital footprint.
- Choosing a Reliable VPN Provider: When selecting a VPN provider, prioritize those with robust encryption standards, a no-logs policy, and transparent privacy practices; this ensures that your data remains secure and your privacy is respected.

9.7 Encryption on the Horizon: Quantum-Resistant Cryptography

The rise of quantum computing poses potential threats to existing encryption methods. Quantum-resistant cryptography emerges as a frontier, exploring algorithms resilient to the computational power of quantum computers.

- Quantum Computing Threats: Quantum computers, once realized, could break widely used encryption algorithms, jeopardizing the security of current digital communication and data protection methods.
- Post-Quantum Cryptography: Post-quantum cryptography aims to develop encryption algorithms resistant to quantum attacks. Ongoing research explores lattice-based cryptography, hash-based cryptography, and other quantum-resistant approaches.
- Transitional Period: As quantum-resistant cryptography evolves, there will be a transitional period during which both traditional and quantum-resistant algorithms coexist. The digital community needs to adapt and implement these advancements proactively.

9.8 The Human Element: Passwords and Two-Factor Authentication (2FA)

While encryption forms an impenetrable barrier around your data, the human element remains a potential vulnerability. Strengthening access controls with secure password practices and two-factor authentication (2FA) bolsters the overall security of your digital accounts.

- Secure Password Practices: Create strong, unique passwords for each account. Avoid easily guessable information and use a password manager to securely generate and store complex passwords.
- Two-Factor Authentication (2FA): 2FA adds an extra layer of security by requiring a second form of verification, such as a code sent to your mobile device and your password; this mitigates the risk of unauthorized access, even if your password is compromised.

9.9 Encryption in Social Media: Protecting Your Digital Persona

Social media platforms, integral to modern communication, often handle vast amounts of personal information. Understanding how encryption operates in social media is crucial for protecting your digital persona.

- End-to-end Encryption in Messaging: Some social media messaging features, like those in Facebook Messenger, offer end-to-end encryption; this ensures that your private conversations remain confidential and secure from unauthorized access.
- Securing Account Access: Implement security features provided by social media platforms, such as login alerts and account recovery options. These measures enhance the overall security of your social media accounts.
- Privacy Settings: Regularly review and adjust privacy settings on your social media profiles. Limiting the visibility of personal information adds an extra layer of defense against potential threats.

9.10 Encryption Education: Empowering the Average Home User

As an average home user navigating the digital landscape, education is your most potent weapon. Familiarizing yourself with encryption concepts and their applications in everyday life empowers you to make informed decisions about your digital security.

- Online Resources and Tutorials: Numerous online resources and tutorials provide accessible information about encryption. Take advantage of these materials to deepen your understanding and enhance your digital literacy.
- Workshops and Webinars: Participate in workshops or webinars conducted by cybersecurity experts or organizations. These events offer practical insights and demonstrations, enriching your knowledge of encryption practices.
- Community Engagement: Engage with online communities focused on digital security and encryption. Discussion forums and social media groups provide platforms for sharing experiences, asking questions, and staying informed about emerging trends.

9.11 The Future of Encryption: Balancing Security and Accessibility

As technology evolves, the future of encryption holds promises and challenges. Striking a balance between robust security measures and user-friendly accessibility remains a focal point for researchers and developers.

- Usability Improvements: Efforts are underway to make encryption tools more user-friendly, ensuring that individuals without extensive technical knowledge can benefit from secure communication and data protection.
- Integration in Everyday Devices: Integrating encryption features in everyday devices, from smartphones to smart home appliances, becomes increasingly important; this trend ensures that privacy and security are embedded in the fabric of our digital lives.
- Global Encryption Policies: Balancing individual privacy rights with law enforcement needs is a complex challenge that requires careful consideration and collaboration.

9.12 Conclusion: Unlocking the Power of Encryption

As we conclude our journey through the realm of encryption, it's essential to recognize the transformative power of this digital lock and key. Encryption empowers you to safeguard your data, communicate securely, and confidently navigate the digital world.

Armed with the knowledge gained in this chapter, you stand as a sentinel, ensuring that your digital interactions remain private and secure. In the upcoming chapters, our cybersecurity exploration continues, unveiling new layers of understanding and equipping you with the tools to fortify your digital defenses against evolving threats.

Chapter 10: The Human Firewall - Educating and Training Your Family

In the intricate dance between cybersecurity threats and defense, the human element remains both the target and the most potent line of defense. This chapter explores the concept of the "Human Firewall" and the critical role your family plays in fortifying the digital defenses of your home. As an average home user, understanding how to educate and train your family members is paramount in creating a resilient and secure digital environment.

10.1 The Human Factor in Cybersecurity

The human element remains a common denominator in the digital landscape, where technology evolves rapidly. Your family members, each with unique digital habits and technological proficiency, collectively form the human firewall that guards against cyber threats.

- Understanding the Human Firewall: The term "human firewall" encapsulates that individuals can act as a protective barrier against cyber threats through awareness, education, and responsible digital practices.

- Common Vulnerabilities: Human vulnerabilities include susceptibility to social engineering, lack of awareness about phishing tactics, and accidental sharing of sensitive information. Recognizing these vulnerabilities is the first step in strengthening the human firewall.

10.2 The Role of Education in Cybersecurity

Education is the cornerstone of a resilient human firewall. Empowering your family members with knowledge about common cyber threats, safe online practices, and the importance of digital hygiene lays the foundation for a secure digital environment.

- Digital Literacy Training: Provide digital literacy training tailored to each family member's individual needs and proficiency levels. Cover essential topics such as recognizing phishing attempts, creating strong passwords, and understanding the risks of various online activities.
- Age-Appropriate Guidance: Tailor your educational approach based on the age of each family member. Younger members may require guidance on safe online gaming. In comparison, older members may benefit from understanding the risks associated with social media and online shopping.
- Interactive Learning: Foster interactive learning experiences to make cybersecurity education engaging and memorable, including interactive workshops, online tutorials, and real-world examples of cyber threats and their consequences.

10.3 Creating a Culture of Security at Home

Building a security culture within your household instills a collective awareness and commitment to digital safety. This cultural shift establishes cybersecurity as a shared responsibility, making it an integral part of your family's daily routine.

- Open Communication: Encourage open communication about cybersecurity within your family. Create an environment where family members feel comfortable discussing potential threats, asking questions, and seeking guidance.
- Lead by Example: As a parent or guardian, lead by example in adopting secure digital practices. Demonstrating responsible behavior, such as using strong passwords, updating software regularly, and being cautious online, sets a powerful precedent.
- Family Cybersecurity Pledges: Consider creating a family cybersecurity pledge that outlines agreed-upon digital practices and responsibilities. This collective commitment reinforces the importance of cybersecurity within your household.

10.4 Recognizing and Mitigating Social Engineering Threats

Social engineering remains a prevalent tactic employed by cybercriminals to exploit human vulnerabilities. It is crucial to educate your family members about the various forms of social engineering and how to recognize and mitigate them.

- Phishing Awareness: Phishing attacks often use deceptive emails, messages, or websites to trick individuals into divulging sensitive information. Teach your family members to recognize phishing attempts, including checking email sender addresses and avoiding clicking on suspicious links.
- Social Media Safety: Discuss the risks of sharing personal information on social media platforms. Emphasize the importance of adjusting privacy settings, being cautious about accepting friend requests, and avoiding sharing sensitive details online.
- Phone Scams and Impersonation: Inform your family about the prevalence of phone scams and impersonation attempts. Remind them only to share personal or financial information over the phone if they can verify the request's legitimacy.

10.5 Password Management for the Whole Family

The strength of passwords is a critical component of digital security. Educate your family members on creating strong, unique passwords and implementing password management practices.

- Password Creation Guidelines: Provide guidelines for creating strong passwords, such as using a mix of uppercase and lowercase letters, numbers, and symbols. Discourage the use of easily guessable information, such as birthdays or names.
- Password Management Tools: Introduce password management tools to help your family members generate, store, and organize complex passwords. These tools streamline the process of maintaining secure credentials for multiple online accounts.
- Regular Password Updates: Emphasize the importance of updating passwords, especially after security breaches or incidents. Encourage family members to use different passwords for each online account to minimize the impact of the potential violations.

10.6 Device Hygiene Practices: From Smartphones to Smart Homes

Digital devices, from smartphones to smart home appliances, are integral to modern living. Using device hygiene ensures your family can navigate the digital landscape safely and securely.

- Software Updates: Emphasize the importance of keeping all devices and applications current. Regular software updates often include security patches that address known vulnerabilities.

- Antivirus and Security Software: Install reputable antivirus and security software on all devices. Ensure that these tools are regularly updated and configured to provide comprehensive protection against malware and other threats.
- Securing Smart Home Devices: If your household includes smart home devices, educate your family about the importance of securing these devices. Change default passwords, update firmware regularly, and be cautious about granting excessive permissions.

10.7 Family-Friendly Online Safety Measures

For families with children, implementing family-friendly online safety measures is paramount. Balancing the benefits of technology with age-appropriate restrictions helps create a safe digital environment for younger family members.

- Parental Controls: Familiarize yourself with and utilize parental control features on devices and online platforms. These controls allow you to set age-appropriate content restrictions, monitor online activities, and establish screen time limits.
- Safe Browsing Practices: Teach younger family members safe browsing practices, including the importance of only visiting reputable websites, avoiding pop-ups, and refraining from downloading content from untrusted sources.
- Online Gaming Safety: If your family engages in online gaming, discuss the potential risks associated with in-game communication and sharing personal information. Encourage responsible gaming behavior and the importance of reporting any inappropriate interactions.

10.8 Two-Factor Authentication (2FA): Layered Security for All

Implementing Two-Factor Authentication (2FA) adds a layer of security to online accounts. Educate your family about the benefits of 2FA and guide them in enabling this feature for their various online accounts.

- Understanding 2FA: Explain the concept of 2FA, which requires users to provide two forms of identification before accessing an account; this often involves a password and a one-time code sent to a mobile device.
- Enabling 2FA: Walk your family members through enabling 2FA on their various online accounts, including email, social media, and financial platforms. Emphasize the added security benefits and the protection against unauthorized access.
- Authentication Apps: Introduce authentication apps, such as Google Authenticator or Authy, as convenient tools for generating 2FA codes. These apps provide an additional layer of security compared to traditional SMS-based codes.

10.9 Cybersecurity Drills and Simulations: From Theory to Practice

Transforming theoretical knowledge into practical skills requires hands-on experience. Conducting cybersecurity drills and simulations within your family creates a proactive approach to handling potential threats.

- Phishing Simulation Exercises: Stage phishing simulation exercises to test your family's ability to recognize and respond to phishing attempts. Please provide feedback and guidance to improve their awareness and resilience against such threats.
- Password Management Challenges: Organize password management challenges, encouraging family members to create and manage secure passwords. This practical approach reinforces the importance of good password hygiene.
- Device Security Checklists: Develop device security checklists that family members can follow to ensure their devices are adequately secured; this may include enabling security features, updating software, and running antivirus scans.

10.10 Addressing Digital Etiquette and Online Behavior

Beyond the technical aspects of cybersecurity, fostering responsible digital etiquette and online behavior contributes to a positive and secure digital environment within your family.

- Respecting Privacy: Instill the importance of respecting each other's privacy online and offline. Discuss the potential consequences of oversharing and the long-term impact of digital footprints.
- Civility in Online Interactions: Teach family members to engage respectfully in online interactions. Emphasize the significance of constructive communication, avoiding cyberbullying, and reporting any inappropriate behavior.
- Balancing Screen Time: Address the issue of excessive screen time and its potential impact on physical and mental well-being. Establish guidelines for balanced screen time, ensuring that technology enhances rather than hinders daily life.

10.11 Navigating Social Media Safely as a Family

Social media has become integral to modern communication, especially for younger generations. Guidance in navigating social media safely ensures that your family members can enjoy the benefits of these platforms while minimizing risks.

- Privacy Settings Review: Regularly review and update privacy settings on social media profiles. Guide family members in adjusting settings to control the visibility of personal information and posts.

- Critical Thinking Skills: Develop critical thinking skills in your family members, empowering them to question the authenticity of information encountered on social media. Encourage fact-checking and responsible sharing practices.
- Reporting Mechanisms: Familiarize your family with the reporting mechanisms available on social media platforms; this includes reporting inappropriate content, blocking or unfriending users, and seeking support from platform administrators.

10.12 Staying Informed: The Ever-Evolving Landscape of Cybersecurity

Cybersecurity is dynamic, with new threats and technologies emerging regularly. Staying informed as a family ensures you can adapt to the evolving landscape and implement proactive security measures.

- Regular Family Security Updates: Schedule regular family discussions or updates on cybersecurity topics. Share insights about emerging threats, new security features, and any relevant changes in digital practices.
- News and Alerts: Stay informed through reputable cybersecurity news sources and alerts. This knowledge equips your family with the awareness to recognize potential threats and respond effectively.
- Community Engagement: Encourage family members to engage with online communities or forums focused on digital security. These platforms provide opportunities to share experiences, ask questions, and learn from the community's collective knowledge.

10.13 Conclusion: Empowering Your Digital Guardians

As you conclude this chapter on educating and training your family as the human firewall, recognize the transformative impact of your efforts. By instilling a culture of security, fostering responsible digital practices, and continuously adapting to the ever-changing landscape of cybersecurity, your family becomes a formidable force against digital threats.

The journey through cybersecurity continues, with each chapter contributing to your understanding and empowerment. In the chapters ahead, we delve deeper into advanced topics, equipping you and your family with the knowledge and tools to navigate the digital world confidently and resiliently.

Chapter 11: Mobile Fortresses - Securing Smart Devices in Your Home

In the interconnected homes and innovative living age, our everyday devices have evolved into intelligent entities that enhance convenience and efficiency. However, with this technological advancement comes the imperative to secure our digital fortresses. This chapter delves into connecting smart devices, transforming your home into a mobile fortress that guards against potential cyber threats. As an average home user, understanding the intricacies of securing these devices is crucial to maintaining a resilient and safe digital environment.

11.1 The Proliferation of Smart Devices

Smart devices have become ubiquitous in modern households, from smart TVs and thermostats to refrigerators and security cameras. These devices offer unparalleled convenience and functionality, but their connectivity introduces potential vulnerabilities that require careful consideration.

- Diverse Ecosystem: The smart home ecosystem encompasses various devices with unique features and connectivity protocols. Understanding the diversity of these devices is the first step in crafting a comprehensive security strategy.
- Connectivity Challenges: Smart devices communicate with each other and the internet, creating a network of interconnected gadgets. This connectivity, while beneficial, also poses challenges in terms of security, as each connected device becomes a potential entry point for cyber threats.

11.2 Understanding Smart Device Vulnerabilities

Smart devices, like any technology, are not immune to vulnerabilities. Recognizing and understanding these vulnerabilities empowers you to address potential security risks proactively.

- Outdated Software: Many smart devices may run on obsolete software that needs the latest security patches. The inability to update firmware leaves these devices susceptible to known vulnerabilities that cybercriminals could exploit.
- Insecure Configurations: Default configurations and passwords set by manufacturers may be insecure or easily guessable. Failing to customize these settings exposes devices to unauthorized access and compromises the overall security of your smart home.
- Lack of Encryption: Some smart devices transmit data in an unencrypted form, making it easier for cybercriminals to intercept and exploit sensitive information. The absence of encryption in communication protocols poses a significant risk to the confidentiality of data.

11.3 Creating a Security Blueprint for Smart Devices

Securing your smart home requires a thoughtful approach that considers the unique characteristics of each device. A security blueprint helps you establish a robust defense against potential cyber threats.

- Device Inventory: Create an inventory of all smart devices in your home; this includes IoT (Internet of Things) devices, smart appliances, and any gadget connected to your home network. Maintain an updated list to track new additions.

- Risk Assessment: Conduct a risk assessment for each smart device. Evaluate the device's security features, update mechanisms, and the manufacturer's reputation for addressing security vulnerabilities. Classify devices based on their risk level.
- Secure Configurations: Customize default settings and passwords on smart devices to enhance security. Use strong, unique passwords for each device, and whenever possible, enable two-factor authentication (2FA) to add a layer of protection.

11.4 Securing Communication Channels

The communication between smart devices and the broader network introduces potential vulnerabilities. Implementing secure communication channels is vital to protecting the integrity and confidentiality of the data transmitted.

- Network Segmentation: Consider segmenting your home network to create isolated zones for smart devices; this helps contain potential breaches and prevents unauthorized access to sensitive areas of your network, such as personal computers.
- Use of Encryption Protocols: Ensure that smart devices communicate over encrypted channels. Utilize protocols like WPA3 for Wi-Fi networks and enable secure communication options provided by individual devices; this safeguards data in transit from interception.
- Regular Network Monitoring: Implement network monitoring tools to track the communication patterns of smart devices. Unusual activities or unexpected connections may indicate a security issue that requires investigation.

11.5 Firmware Updates and Patch Management

Regularly updating firmware and managing patches are fundamental practices for maintaining the security of smart devices. Manufacturers release updates to address vulnerabilities and enhance overall device security.

- Automated Updates: Enable automatic updates whenever possible; this ensures that devices receive the latest security patches promptly, reducing the window of vulnerability. Check manufacturer guidelines to understand the update process for each device.
- Scheduled Audits: Conduct regular audits of smart devices to verify their firmware versions. Establish a schedule for these audits and promptly address any devices that require updates. Consider using centralized management tools for efficiency.
- Vendor Accountability: Choose smart devices from reputable manufacturers with a track record of timely security updates. Prioritize devices that provide long-term support, reducing the risk of using outdated or unsupported hardware.

11.6 Implementing Access Controls

Controlling access to smart devices is essential for preventing unauthorized usage and potential exploitation by cybercriminals. Implementing access controls enhances the overall security posture of your smart home.

- User Account Management: Create unique user accounts for each family member interacting with smart devices. Avoid using default or shared accounts, as this simplifies access control and enables activity tracking for individual users.
- Role-Based Access: Assign roles and permissions based on user responsibilities. For example, limit access to critical smart devices, such as security cameras or door locks, to specific individuals; this minimizes the risk of accidental or intentional misuse.
- Regular Access Reviews: Regularly review user accounts and their associated access permissions. Remove any unnecessary accounts and adjust permissions as needed. This practice ensures that only authorized individuals can control and monitor smart devices.

11.7 Physical Security Measures

The physical security of smart devices is often overlooked but is crucial in preventing unauthorized access or tampering. Implementing physical security measures adds an extra layer of protection to your smart home.

- Secure Device Placement: Place smart devices in locations that prevent physical tampering. For example, position security cameras out of reach and secure smart home hubs in inaccessible areas.
- Device Tamper Alerts: Some smart devices come equipped with tamper detection features. Enable these alerts to receive notifications if a device is physically tampered with, allowing you to respond promptly to potential security breaches.
- Secure IoT Devices: For outdoor smart devices, such as smart locks or garage door openers, ensure they are built to withstand environmental conditions. Choose devices with durable and weather-resistant designs to maintain functionality and security.

11.8 Securing Smart Cameras and Privacy Concerns

Smart cameras are prevalent in modern smart homes, providing security and convenience. However, these devices raise privacy concerns, and securing them requires careful consideration of both technical and ethical aspects.

- Camera Placement and Privacy Zones: Strategically position smart cameras to capture essential areas while respecting the privacy of your family members and neighbors. Most smart cameras allow the creation of privacy zones to exclude specific areas from recording.
- Strong Authentication: Implement robust authentication mechanisms for accessing smart camera feeds. Use unique, complex passwords and enable two-factor authentication to prevent unauthorized access to live camera streams.
- Local Storage Options: Consider smart cameras with local storage options, such as microSD cards or network-attached storage (NAS); this reduces reliance on cloud storage and provides more control over the storage and access to recorded footage.

11.9 Safeguarding Voice-Activated Assistants

Voice-activated assistants, such as smart speakers, have become integral to many smart homes. While convenient, these devices raise privacy and security considerations that merit attention.

- Privacy Settings: Review and adjust privacy settings on voice-activated assistants. Understand the data collection practices of the manufacturer and choose settings that align with your comfort level regarding the recording and storage of voice commands.
- Voice Recognition Security: Enable voice recognition features to enhance security. Some devices can learn and recognize the voices of authorized users, limiting access to personal information and preventing unauthorized commands.
- Regular Security Audits: Periodically review the security settings of voice-activated assistants. Ensure the device runs the latest firmware, and check for any unauthorized connected devices or activities.

11.10 The Challenge of IoT Device Diversity

The Internet of Things (IoT) encompasses various devices with unique functionalities and security considerations. Managing the diversity of IoT devices in your smart home requires a comprehensive and adaptable approach.

- Standardization Efforts: Stay informed about industry standardization efforts in the IoT space. Standards and protocols designed to enhance the interoperability and security of IoT devices can guide your choices when adding new devices to your smart home.
- Manufacturer Collaboration: Choose devices from manufacturers that actively collaborate with the broader IoT ecosystem. Manufacturers committed to security and interoperability are more likely to provide ongoing product support and updates.

- IoT Security Platforms: Explore IoT security platforms that offer centralized management and monitoring of diverse devices. These platforms can provide a unified interface for securing and controlling various IoT devices in your smart home.

11.11 Cybersecurity Hygiene for Smart Homes
Adopting good cybersecurity hygiene practices is integral to maintaining the overall security of your smart home. Consistent and mindful efforts contribute to a safer and more resilient digital living environment.

- Regular Security Audits: Conduct regular security audits of your smart home devices; this includes reviewing settings, checking for software updates, and ensuring that security features are configured appropriately.
- Incident Response Planning: Develop an incident response plan specific to smart home security. Outline steps to take in the event of a security breach, including isolating affected devices, contacting manufacturers for support, and updating passwords.
- User Education and Awareness: Educate all household members about the security implications of smart devices. Foster an awareness of potential threats and the importance of responsible usage to create a culture of cybersecurity within your family.

11.12 Future Trends in Smart Device Security
As technology advances, so do the strategies employed by cybercriminals. Anticipating future trends in smart device security allows you to adapt your cybersecurity measures to emerging challenges proactively.

- Edge Computing for Smart Devices: The adoption of edge computing for smart devices is rising. This approach processes data locally on the device, reducing the reliance on cloud services and minimizing data exposure.
- Blockchain for Device Authentication: Blockchain technology shows promise in enhancing device authentication and security. Decentralized identity management and secure transactions could contribute to a more robust security framework for smart devices.
- AI-Driven Threat Detection: Artificial Intelligence (AI) is increasingly utilized for threat detection in smart homes. AI algorithms can analyze device behavior patterns to identify anomalies and potential security threats, enhancing overall cybersecurity.

11.13 Conclusion: Fortifying Your Mobile Fortress
As we conclude our exploration of securing smart devices in your home, envision your dwelling as a mobile fortress fortified against cyber threats. By understanding the vulnerabilities of smart devices,

implementing robust security measures, and staying attuned to evolving trends, you empower yourself as the guardian of your digital realm.

The journey through the intricate cybersecurity landscape continues, with each chapter contributing to your knowledge and resilience. In the forthcoming chapters, we explore advanced concepts, equipping you with the tools to navigate the digital frontier with confidence and sophistication.

Chapter 12: Incident Response - What to Do When the Walls Are Breached

In the ever-evolving landscape of cybersecurity, the reality is that even the most fortified digital fortresses may face breaches. Incidents can range from a suspicious email compromising your accounts to a more severe scenario involving unauthorized access to your home network. This chapter is your guide to incident response, outlining the steps and strategies to take when the walls of your digital fortress are breached. As an average home user, understanding how to respond to incidents effectively is crucial for minimizing damage and restoring the security of your digital domain.

12.1 The Nature of Cybersecurity Incidents

Before delving into the intricacies of incident response, it's essential to comprehend the diverse nature of cybersecurity incidents that could impact your home network. These incidents can be categorized into several types:

- Malware Infections: The infiltration of malicious software, such as viruses, ransomware, or spyware, into your devices or network.
- Unauthorized Access: Breaches where an attacker gains unauthorized access to your accounts, devices, or home network.
- Phishing Attacks: Deceptive attempts to trick individuals into divulging sensitive information, often through fraudulent emails or messages.
- Data Breaches: Unauthorized access or exposure of sensitive personal information, potentially leading to identity theft or financial harm.
- Device Compromise: Instances where attackers gain control over your smart devices, such as security cameras or smart home hubs.

12.2 Building a Foundation: Incident Response Plan

An effective incident response begins with preparation. Developing an incident response plan lays the groundwork for a structured and organized approach when facing cybersecurity incidents.

- Incident Response Team: Identify individuals within your household who will be part of the incident response team, including family members with technical expertise or those responsible for coordinating communication and decision-making.
- Contact Information: Compile a list of essential contact information, including relevant support channels for your internet service provider, device manufacturers, and any other services you may need during an incident.
- Incident Categories: Categorize potential incidents based on severity. This classification helps prioritize responses, ensuring that critical incidents receive immediate attention.

12.3 Recognizing the Signs of an Incident

Timely detection is a critical aspect of effective incident response. Recognizing the signs of a cybersecurity incident allows you to respond promptly and mitigate potential damage.

- Unusual Device Behavior: Monitor the behavior of your devices regularly. Unexpected slowdowns, frequent crashes, or unusual network activity may indicate a potential incident.
- Unauthorized Access Alerts: If your devices or accounts provide alerts for unauthorized access attempts, take these notifications seriously. Investigate any login attempts that you did not initiate.
- Unexplained Changes: Sudden changes in device settings, the appearance of unfamiliar files, or account information modifications may signal a security incident.

12.4 Immediate Response: Containment and Isolation

Upon recognizing signs of a cybersecurity incident, swift action is necessary to contain the threat and prevent further damage. The critical elements of immediate response include:

- Disconnecting Compromised Devices: If a specific device is compromised, disconnect it from the network immediately; this helps prevent the spread of malware or unauthorized access.
- Changing Passwords: Change the passwords for compromised accounts promptly. Use strong, unique passwords for each account, and consider enabling two-factor authentication for added security.

12.5 Investigation and Analysis: Understanding the Incident

Once the immediate threats are contained, the next phase involves a thorough investigation to understand the nature and scope of the incident.

- Forensic Analysis: Conduct a forensic analysis of affected devices; this involves examining logs, system files, and network traffic to determine the origin and extent of the incident.

- Identifying the Attack Vector: Determine how the incident occurred. Was it a result of a phishing email, a malware download, or an exploited vulnerability in a device or software?
- Timeline Reconstruction: Create a timeline of events leading up to and during the incident; this helps understand the sequence of actions taken by the attacker and aids in crafting a more effective incident response strategy.

12.6 Communication Strategy: Transparency and Collaboration

Clear communication is vital during a cybersecurity incident. Keep in mind the following considerations when communicating about the incident:

- Internal Communication: Maintain open and transparent communication within your incident response team. Ensure that everyone is informed about the incident's current status and any investigation findings.
- External Communication: If the incident involves potential risks to others, such as friends, family, or contacts, consider communicating relevant information; this fosters a collaborative approach to addressing the incident.
- Service Providers and Authorities: Report the incident to relevant service providers, such as your internet service provider or device manufacturers. If the incident involves illegal activities, consider contacting law enforcement authorities.

12.7 Remediation and Recovery: Restoring Normalcy

With a clear understanding of the incident, the focus shifts to remediation and recovery. The objective is to eliminate the incident's root cause and restore normal operations.

- Device and Software Updates: Ensure all devices and software are updated to the latest versions. Applying patches and updates addresses known vulnerabilities and strengthens the overall security posture.
- Rebuilding Compromised Systems: In compromised devices, consider rebuilding or restoring them to a known good state; this may involve reinstalling operating systems and applications.
- Password Changes and Monitoring: Continue to monitor accounts for any unusual activities. Periodically change passwords, especially after an incident, to reduce the risk of persistent unauthorized access.

12.8 Post-Incident Review: Learning for the Future

Concluding the incident response process involves a comprehensive review of the incident and the actions taken. The post-incident review is instrumental in learning from the experience and improving your cybersecurity posture.

- Identifying Gaps in Security: Evaluate the incident response process to identify gaps or weaknesses. This assessment helps refine your incident response plan for future incidents.
- Updating Incident Response Plan: Incorporate lessons learned into your incident response plan; this may involve updating contact information, refining communication strategies, or adjusting the categorization of incident severity.
- Continuous Improvement: Recognize incident response as an ongoing process of constant improvement. Regularly review and update your incident response plan to adapt to emerging threats and changes in your digital environment.

12.9 Seeking Professional Assistance

Cybersecurity incidents may sometimes be complex or sophisticated, requiring professional assistance. Consider seeking help from cybersecurity experts or professional services to:

- Conduct a Thorough Investigation: Professionals can bring expertise in forensic analysis, helping uncover the full extent of the incident and identify potential vulnerabilities.
- Implement Advanced Security Measures: Cybersecurity professionals can recommend and implement advanced security measures tailored to your specific digital environment, reducing the risk of future incidents.
- Provide Legal Guidance: If the incident involves legal implications, such as identity theft or financial fraud, consulting with legal professionals can guide you on the appropriate actions.

12.10 Conclusion: Building Resilience Through Experience

Navigating a cybersecurity incident can be a challenging experience, but it also provides an opportunity to strengthen your digital resilience. By following a well-defined incident response plan, promptly containing threats, and learning from the experience, you position yourself as a more capable guardian of your digital domain.

As we conclude this chapter on incident response, remember that cybersecurity is an evolving landscape. The knowledge and experience gained through each incident contribute to your ongoing journey as a vigilant and empowered user. In the upcoming chapters, we delve into advanced topics, further equipping you with the tools and insights to navigate the dynamic realm of cybersecurity with confidence and effectiveness.

Chapter 13: Into the Future - Emerging Threats and Technologies

As we venture into the future, the cybersecurity landscape continues evolving, presenting new threats and innovative technologies. Staying ahead of the curve is essential for the average home user as the digital frontier transforms and introduces challenges that demand awareness and adaptability. This chapter explores the emerging threats on the horizon and the technologies shaping the future of cybersecurity, providing insights to help you confidently navigate the ever-changing digital landscape.

13.1 The Shifting Landscape of Cybersecurity

The digital realm is in a constant state of flux, and understanding the evolving nature of cybersecurity is crucial for preparing against emerging threats. Here are some critical aspects of the shifting cybersecurity landscape:

- Increased Connectivity: The proliferation of IoT devices, smart homes, and interconnected technologies amplifies the attack surface, offering more entry points for cyber threats.
- Sophisticated Threat Actors: Cybercriminals continue to advance their tactics, techniques, and procedures with increasing sophistication. Threat actors range from individual hackers to well-organized cybercrime syndicates.
- Ransomware Evolution: Ransomware attacks have evolved beyond simple encryption of files to include data exfiltration and double extortion, making them more financially lucrative for attackers.
- Privacy Concerns: The growing concern for digital privacy, driven by increased data collection and surveillance practices, prompts reevaluating how personal information is handled and protected.

13.2 Emerging Cybersecurity Threats

In the ever-changing cybersecurity landscape, new threats continually emerge, challenging the defenses of individuals and organizations alike. Understanding these threats is pivotal for implementing effective security measures. Here are some emerging cybersecurity threats to be aware of:

- AI-Powered Attacks: The use of artificial intelligence (AI) by cybercriminals to automate and enhance the efficiency of attacks, making them more targeted and evasive.
- 5G Vulnerabilities: The rollout of 5G technology introduces new vulnerabilities, potentially increasing the attack surface and providing threat actors with faster and more reliable means of communication.
- Deepfake Dangers: Deepfake technology, which creates compelling fake videos or audio recordings, poses risks regarding misinformation, identity theft, and social engineering attacks.
- Supply Chain Attacks: Targeting vulnerabilities within the supply chain, cybercriminals aim to compromise products or services before they reach end-users, posing significant risks to businesses and individuals.

- Biometric Data Exploitation: As biometric authentication grows, so does the risk of biometric data being targeted for exploitation, potentially leading to unauthorized access and identity theft.

13.3 Advanced Authentication Technologies

In response to the evolving threat landscape, authentication technologies are advancing to provide more robust and secure methods of verifying identity. As an average home user, staying informed about these technologies can enhance the security of your digital accounts:

- Biometric Authentication: Utilizing unique physical or behavioral traits, such as fingerprints or facial recognition, for secure and convenient access to devices and accounts.
- Behavioral Biometrics: Analyzing user behavior patterns, such as typing speed and mouse movements, to create a unique profile for authentication purposes.
- Multi-Factor Authentication (MFA): Combining two or more authentication factors, such as passwords, biometrics, and one-time codes, to add an extra layer of security.
- Universal Second Factor (U2F): Physical security keys that provide an additional layer of protection, particularly effective against phishing attacks.

13.4 Artificial Intelligence in Cybersecurity

As artificial intelligence becomes more prevalent, it is being leveraged to enhance cybersecurity measures. AI offers the potential to analyze vast amounts of data, identify patterns, and detect anomalies more efficiently than traditional methods:

- Behavioral Analysis: AI-driven behavioral analysis can identify unusual activity patterns on networks or devices, signaling potential security threats.
- Threat Intelligence: AI can process and analyze large datasets to provide real-time threat intelligence, helping organizations and individuals stay informed about emerging threats.
- Automated Threat Detection and Response: AI-powered systems can autonomously detect and respond to security incidents, reducing the response time and mitigating the impact of attacks.
- Adversarial Machine Learning: As AI is used for defense, cybercriminals are also exploring ways to exploit AI systems through adversarial machine learning, creating challenges in maintaining the integrity of AI-driven security measures.

13.5 Privacy-Preserving Technologies

With growing concerns about digital privacy, technologies prioritizing protecting personal information are gaining importance. As an average home user, understanding and adopting these privacy-preserving technologies can empower you to take control of your digital footprint:

- Zero-Knowledge Proofs: Cryptographic methods that allow one party to prove the authenticity of information without revealing the actual data, ensuring privacy in transactions and communications.
- Privacy-Focused Browsers: Browsers are designed with enhanced privacy features, such as blocking trackers and minimizing data collection, to provide a more private online browsing experience.
- Decentralized Identity: Systems that enable individuals to control and manage their digital identities without relying on centralized authorities, enhancing privacy and reducing the risk of identity theft.
- End-to-end Encryption: Encrypting data so that only the intended recipient can decrypt and access it, ensuring that communication remains confidential and secure.

13.6 Quantum Computing and Cybersecurity

The development of quantum computing introduces both opportunities and challenges for cybersecurity. While quantum computers have the potential to break specific cryptographic algorithms, new cryptographic methods are being explored to resist quantum attacks:

- Quantum Key Distribution (QKD): A method that uses quantum properties to secure communication channels, making it theoretically immune to interception or eavesdropping.
- Post-Quantum Cryptography: Developing cryptographic algorithms resistant to attacks by classical and quantum computers, ensuring long-term security in the post-quantum era.
- Quantum-Safe Encryption: Implementing encryption techniques that can withstand attacks from quantum computers, safeguarding data against potential quantum threats.

13.7 Cybersecurity Education and Awareness

As the digital landscape evolves, cybersecurity education and awareness become increasingly crucial. Empowering individuals with the knowledge to recognize and respond to potential threats is a fundamental aspect of building a resilient digital community:

- User Training Programs: Providing educational resources and training programs to help individuals recognize phishing attempts, practice secure online behaviors, and understand the importance of cybersecurity.
- Community Engagement: Fostering a sense of community awareness and collaboration to share information about emerging threats, best practices, and cybersecurity-related experiences.
- Government Initiatives: Governments and regulatory bodies promote cybersecurity education through initiatives that raise awareness, set standards, and enforce cybersecurity practices.

13.8 Cybersecurity for Smart Cities and Homes

Integrating technology into urban environments, known as smart cities, poses unique cybersecurity challenges. As homes become more intelligent and more connected, it's essential to consider the implications and implement security measures:

- Smart City Infrastructure Security: Protecting critical infrastructure, such as energy grids, transportation systems, and communication networks, from cyber threats that could impact the functioning of an entire city.
- Security Standards for IoT Devices: Establish and adhere to security standards for IoT devices in smart homes to ensure they resist cyber-attacks and do not pose risks to the broader network.
- Collaboration Between Stakeholders: Encouraging cooperation between city planners, technology developers, and cybersecurity experts to effectively address the challenges of securing smart cities and homes.

13.9 Conclusion: Navigating the Uncharted Terrain

As we peer into the future of cybersecurity, the terrain ahead is challenging and promising. Emerging threats demand vigilance, while innovative technologies offer new avenues for protection. As an average home user, embracing a proactive approach to cybersecurity, staying informed about the latest developments, and adopting security measures can empower you to navigate the uncharted terrain of the digital future with confidence and resilience.

In the upcoming chapters, we delve deeper into advanced strategies and concepts, equipping you with the knowledge and tools needed to fortify your digital fortress against the evolving challenges of the cybersecurity landscape.

Chapter 14: Community Watch - Online Safety Beyond Your Home

Cybersecurity extends beyond individual homes to encompass the broader digital community in our interconnected world. This chapter explores the importance of a community watch approach to online safety, emphasizing collaboration, awareness, and shared responsibility among average home users. As we navigate the intricacies of the digital realm, understanding the significance of community-wide cybersecurity practices becomes essential for fostering a safer online environment for everyone.

14.1 The Interconnected Web: Understanding Digital Community Dynamics

The internet is not just a collection of isolated individuals but a vast digital community where actions ripple across networks, affecting users far beyond individual households. Recognizing the interconnected nature of the online world lays the foundation for a community watch approach to cybersecurity:

- Shared Digital Spaces: Social media platforms, online forums, and collaborative spaces create shared digital environments where one user's actions can impact others' experiences.
- Global Threat Landscape: Cyber threats know no borders and a vulnerability in one part of the world can be exploited to affect users globally. Collaboration is critical to addressing these shared challenges.
- Collective Responsibility: In a digital community, users contribute to the overall security posture. By promoting a sense of collective responsibility, users can actively contribute to the safety of their digital spaces.

14.2 The Role of Digital Literacy in Community Cybersecurity

Digital literacy is the cornerstone of a community watch approach to cybersecurity. Empowering individuals with the knowledge and skills to navigate the digital landscape safely enhances the overall resilience of the digital community:

- Recognizing Phishing Attempts: Educating community members about the common signs of phishing emails and messages helps create a collective defense against deceptive tactics employed by cybercriminals.
- Understanding Online Privacy: Providing resources on safeguarding personal information, using privacy settings effectively, and recognizing potential privacy risks enhances the community's digital literacy.
- Promoting Secure Password Practices: Encouraging the use of strong, unique passwords and the adoption of multi-factor authentication contributes to the overall security of the community.
- Navigating Social Media Safely: Providing guidance on responsible social media usage, understanding privacy settings, and recognizing potential risks of sharing personal information online.

14.3 Building a Digital Neighborhood Watch

Just as neighborhoods have watchful residents contributing to the safety of the physical community, the digital landscape benefits from a collective effort. Establishing a digital neighborhood watch involves fostering communication, collaboration, and information-sharing:

- Online Forums and Groups: Creating online spaces where community members can share cybersecurity tips, report suspicious activities, and seek assistance fosters a sense of community vigilance.
- Community Awareness Campaigns: Initiating campaigns that raise awareness about emerging cyber threats, best practices for online safety, and the importance of reporting incidents contributes to the overall digital well-being of the community.
- Local Cybersecurity Events: Organizing events such as webinars, workshops, or community forums focusing on cybersecurity encourages dialogue and collaboration among community members.
- Collaboration with Local Authorities: Establishing communication channels with local law enforcement, cybersecurity organizations, and relevant authorities enhances the community's ability to respond effectively to cyber incidents.

14.4 Reporting and Responding to Cyber Incidents

In a digital community, reporting and responding to cyber incidents promptly is paramount. Encouraging a culture of reporting and providing resources for effective incident response strengthens the resilience of the digital neighborhood watch:

- Clear Reporting Channels: Establishing clear channels for reporting cyber incidents, such as suspicious emails, phishing attempts, or malware infections, ensures community members can seek assistance when needed.
- Incident Response Resources: Providing accessible resources that guide community members through incident response, including containment, isolation, and reporting to relevant authorities.
- Community Support Networks: Creating networks where community members can support those affected by cyber incidents, share recovery strategies, and collectively learn from shared experiences.
- Collaboration with Cybersecurity Professionals: For more complex incidents, fostering collaboration with local cybersecurity professionals or organizations can provide expert assistance in investigating and mitigating threats.

14.5 Empowering the Next Generation: Cybersecurity Education in Schools

Building a resilient digital community requires an investment in the cybersecurity education of the next generation. Integrating cybersecurity education into schools equips young learners with the knowledge and skills necessary to navigate the digital landscape safely:

- Incorporating Cybersecurity Curriculum: Collaborating with educational institutions to integrate cybersecurity topics into the curriculum, teaching students about online safety, responsible internet use, and basic cybersecurity principles.
- Student-led Cybersecurity Initiatives: Encouraging student-led initiatives, such as cybersecurity clubs or awareness campaigns, empowers young individuals to promote a culture of cybersecurity actively within their communities.
- Engaging Parents and Guardians: Extending cybersecurity education beyond the classroom by involving parents and guardians in awareness programs, ensuring a holistic approach to online safety for students at home and in school.

14.6 Addressing Digital Inclusion and Accessibility

A genuinely resilient digital community is inclusive, ensuring that all members, regardless of background or ability, can participate safely in the online environment. Addressing digital inclusion and accessibility involves:

- Promoting Inclusive Practices: Encouraging inclusive language and practices that consider diverse perspectives, backgrounds, and abilities in the digital community, fostering an environment where everyone feels welcome and supported.
- Accessibility in Cybersecurity Education: Ensuring that cybersecurity education materials and resources are accessible to individuals with diverse learning needs, promoting equal participation in community watch initiatives.
- Support for Vulnerable Populations: Recognizing that certain groups may be more vulnerable to cyber threats and providing targeted support and resources to address their unique cybersecurity challenges.

14.7 Collaboration with Local Businesses and Organizations

Local businesses and organizations play a pivotal role in the digital ecosystem in many communities. Collaborating with these entities enhances the overall cybersecurity posture of the community:

- Sharing Threat Intelligence: Establishing channels for sharing threat intelligence and best practices between local businesses and community members enhances the collective ability to respond to evolving cyber threats.
- Supporting Small Businesses: Providing resources and guidance to small businesses on implementing effective cybersecurity measures ensures the resilience of the broader community against cyber threats that may target local enterprises.

- Community Cybersecurity Events: Coordinating cybersecurity events that involve local businesses, community organizations, and residents fosters a sense of shared responsibility and collaboration in safeguarding the digital environment.

14.8 Privacy Advocacy in the Digital Community

Privacy is a fundamental aspect of online safety, and advocating for privacy rights within the digital community contributes to a safer and more secure online environment:

- Privacy Awareness Campaigns: Launch campaigns that educate community members about their digital privacy rights, the importance of consent, and ways to protect personal information online.
- Privacy-Centric Tools and Practices: Encouraging the adoption of privacy-centric tools and practices within the community, such as encrypted communication platforms and privacy-focused browser settings.
- Supporting Privacy Legislation: Advocating for and supporting privacy-focused legislation that protects individuals' digital rights and holds organizations accountable for responsible data practices.

14.9 Cybersecurity Challenges Unique to Community Environments

While the concept of a digital neighborhood watch is empowering, it comes with challenges. Understanding and addressing these challenges is crucial for building a resilient and practical community approach to online safety:

- Diversity of Digital Environments: Recognizing that community members may use different devices, operating systems, and online platforms requires flexibility in cybersecurity practices and recommendations.
- Varied Technical Proficiency: Acknowledging the diverse technical proficiency levels within the community and tailoring cybersecurity education and resources to meet the needs of users with varying levels of expertise.
- Balancing Security and Usability: Striking a balance between implementing strong security measures and ensuring that they do not create barriers to accessibility or hinder the usability of digital tools.

14.10 Conclusion: Strengthening the Digital Tapestry

In the digital age, the strength of the entire tapestry depends on each individual thread's resilience. By embracing the concept of a community watch for online safety, average home users contribute to a collective defense that extends beyond their personal digital fortresses. As we conclude this chapter, remember that the power of community lies in collaboration, shared awareness, and the understanding that online safety is a shared responsibility.

In the final chapter, we delve into the overarching principles that tie together the diverse aspects of cybersecurity for home users. From foundational practices to advanced strategies, this comprehensive guide equips you with the knowledge and tools to navigate cybersecurity's dynamic and ever-evolving landscape with confidence and resilience.

Chapter 15: Fortifying the Future - Cybersecurity Practices for Tomorrow

As we stand at the threshold of the future, cybersecurity continues to evolve, presenting challenges and opportunities for average home users. This concluding chapter is a comprehensive guide to fortifying your digital defenses for the days ahead. We delve into advanced cybersecurity practices, emerging technologies, and proactive strategies to empower you in navigating the dynamic landscape of tomorrow's digital frontier.

15.1 Adaptive Cybersecurity: Navigating the Dynamic Landscape
The pace at which technology evolves demands a shift from static security measures to adaptive cybersecurity practices. Adaptive cybersecurity involves continuous learning, proactive adjustments, and a dynamic approach to counter the ever-changing threat landscape:

- Continuous Learning: Stay informed about cybersecurity threats, trends, and technologies. Engage with online resources, attend webinars, and participate in communities to stay abreast of the dynamic cybersecurity landscape.
- Proactive Adjustments: Recognize cybersecurity as an ongoing process requiring regular assessments and adjustments. Be proactive in updating security measures, patching vulnerabilities, and adapting to emerging threats.
- Dynamic Threat Response: Develop a mindset of dynamic threat response. Instead of relying on fixed security measures, be prepared to adapt your cybersecurity strategy based on the evolving nature of cyber threats.

15.2 Advanced Password Practices: Beyond the Basics
While solid passwords remain a fundamental aspect of cybersecurity, advanced practices can further enhance your account security. Consider the following strategies to fortify your password management:

- Password Managers: Explore the use of reputable password manager tools. These tools generate complex, unique passwords for each account and securely store them, reducing the risk of password reuse.
- Biometric Authentication: Where available, leverage biometric authentication methods such as fingerprint or facial recognition. These add a layer of security to your devices and accounts.
- Password Rotation: Implement a regular password rotation policy, especially for critical accounts. Changing passwords periodically reduces the risk of compromise, even if a password is inadvertently exposed.

15.3 Zero Trust Security Model: Verifying Every Access Attempt

The Zero Trust security model is gaining prominence as a robust approach to cybersecurity. In a Zero Trust environment, trust is never assumed, and verification is required from everyone, whether inside or outside the network:

- Micro-Segmentation: Implement micro-segmentation to divide your network into smaller, isolated segments; this limits lateral movement for potential attackers, enhancing the overall security posture.
- Continuous Authentication: Move beyond traditional authentication methods and explore continuous authentication; this involves ongoing verification throughout a user's session, reducing the risk of unauthorized access.
- Least Privilege Access: Adhere to the principle of least privilege, granting users and devices only the minimum level of access necessary to perform their functions; this minimizes the impact of potential breaches.

15.4 AI-Driven Threat Detection: Enhancing Incident Response

Artificial Intelligence (AI) is becoming a crucial ally in threat detection and incident response. By harnessing the power of AI, home users can benefit from more advanced and efficient security measures:

- Behavioral Analytics: Implement AI-driven behavioral analytics to detect abnormal patterns of activity. This technology can identify potential threats based on deviations from established user behavior.
- Automated Incident Response: Explore using AI to automate certain aspects of incident response. Automated systems can quickly detect and respond to known threats, reducing the response time and minimizing damage.

- Threat Intelligence Integration: Leverage AI to integrate threat intelligence into your security measures. AI can analyze vast datasets to identify emerging threats, providing a proactive defense against the latest cyber risks.

15.5 Secure Home Automation: IoT Best Practices

Securing smart devices is paramount as the Internet of Things (IoT) becomes more integrated into our homes. Apply best practices to ensure the security of your home automation ecosystem:

- Change Default Credentials: Immediately change default usernames and passwords on IoT devices. Default credentials are often well-known and can be exploited by attackers.
- Regular Firmware Updates: Keep all IoT devices updated with the latest firmware. Manufacturers release updates to address vulnerabilities, and staying current is essential for maintaining security.
- Network Segmentation: Segment your home network to isolate IoT devices from critical systems; this limits the potential impact of a compromised IoT device on the overall security of your network.

15.6 Quantum-Resistant Cryptography: Preparing for the Post-Quantum Era

With the advent of quantum computing, traditional cryptographic methods face potential vulnerabilities. Consider adopting quantum-resistant cryptography to future-proof your digital communications:

- Post-Quantum Algorithms: Stay informed about developments in post-quantum cryptography and consider adopting algorithms resistant to attacks from classical and quantum computers.
- Quantum Key Distribution: Explore Quantum Key Distribution (QKD) for securing communication channels. QKD leverages quantum properties to provide a theoretically secure method of key exchange.
- Stay Informed: As quantum computing advances, stay informed about the latest developments in quantum-resistant cryptography. Regularly assess the security of your cryptographic practices in light of emerging threats.

15.7 Privacy-Preserving Technologies: Safeguarding Personal Information

Integrating privacy-preserving technologies into your online activities becomes crucial as digital privacy concerns grow. Explore the following practices to protect your personal information:

- Anonymous Browsing: Use privacy-focused browsers or activate private browsing modes to limit the collection of browsing history and cookies.

- Encrypted Communication: Opt for encrypted communication channels, especially for sensitive information. End-to-end encryption ensures that only the intended recipient can access the communicated data.
- Blockchain for Privacy: Investigate the use of blockchain technology for specific applications. Blockchain provides a decentralized and tamper-resistant approach to data storage and transactions.

15.8 Cybersecurity Education for All Ages: A Lifelong Journey

Cybersecurity education is not a one-time effort; it's a lifelong journey. Regardless of age or experience level, ongoing education is critical to maintaining a strong cybersecurity posture:

- Family Education Programs: Engage in family education programs that promote online safety for all members. These programs can cover topics such as safe internet usage, recognizing phishing attempts, and protecting personal information.
- Cybersecurity Games and Simulations: Explore educational games and simulations that make learning about cybersecurity enjoyable. These tools are particularly effective for teaching children and teenagers about online safety.
- Community Workshops and Webinars: Attend community workshops and webinars focusing on cybersecurity. These events provide opportunities to learn from experts, share experiences, and stay updated on the latest developments.

15.9 Cybersecurity Resilience Planning: Beyond Incident Response

While incident response is crucial, building a comprehensive cybersecurity resilience plan involves proactive measures to prevent, detect, and respond to cyber threats effectively:

- Regular Security Audits: Conduct regular security audits to identify vulnerabilities in your digital environment. Addressing these vulnerabilities before they can be exploited enhances overall cybersecurity resilience.
- Tabletop Exercises: Engage in tabletop exercises that simulate various cybersecurity scenarios. These exercises help you practice responding to potential incidents and refine your incident response plan.
- Collaboration with ISPs and Security Providers: Collaborate with your Internet Service Provider (ISP) and security providers to enhance your cybersecurity defenses. Many ISPs offer security features, and partnering with them can provide additional protection.

15.10 Sustainability in Cybersecurity: Minimizing Environmental Impact

As we look to the future, considering the environmental impact of our digital activities becomes increasingly important. Adopt sustainable cybersecurity practices to minimize your carbon footprint:

- Energy-Efficient Devices: Choose energy-efficient devices and technologies for your digital ecosystem; this reduces your environmental impact and lowers your energy bills.
- E-Waste Management: Responsibly dispose of electronic waste (e-waste) by recycling or donating old devices; this helps prevent environmental pollution and encourages a circular economy for electronic products.
- Carbon-Aware Computing: Be mindful of the carbon footprint associated with your digital activities. Consider using tools and platforms that prioritize energy efficiency and environmental sustainability.

15.11 Conclusion: Embracing the Future with Confidence

In the ever-evolving cybersecurity landscape, the journey doesn't end; it transforms. By adopting advanced practices, staying informed about emerging technologies, and fostering a proactive mindset, you fortify your digital fortress for the challenges of tomorrow.

As we conclude this comprehensive guide, remember that cybersecurity is not just a set of practices; it's a mindset—a commitment to securing your digital presence and contributing to the collective defense of the online community. Embrace the future with confidence, equipped with the knowledge and resilience to navigate cybersecurity's dynamic and ever-changing landscape. The digital frontier awaits, and you stand prepared to face it with strength and assurance.